The Rifleman

TV Milestones

Series Editors

Barry Keith Grant
Brock University

Jeanette Sloniowski
Brock University

TV Milestones is part of the Contemporary Approaches to Film and Television Series

A complete listing of the books in this series can be found online at *http://wsupress.wayne.edu*

General Editor

Barry Keith Grant
Brock University

Advisory Editors

Patricia B. Erens
School of the Art Institute
 of Chicago

Lucy Fischer
University of Pittsburgh

Peter Lehman
Arizona State University

Caren J. Deming
University of Arizona

Robert J. Burgoyne
Wayne State University

Tom Gunning
University of Chicago

Anna McCarthy
New York University

Peter X. Feng
University of Delaware

THE RIFLEMAN

Christopher Sharrett

TV MILESTONES SERIES

Wayne State University Press | Detroit

© 2005 by Wayne State University Press,

Detroit, Michigan 48201. All rights reserved.

No part of this book may be reproduced without formal permission.

Manufactured in the United States of America.

09 08 07 06 05   5 4 3 2 1

Library of Congress Cataloging-in-Publication Data

Sharrett, Christopher.
The Rifleman / Christopher Sharrett.
       p. cm. — (Contemporary approaches to film and television series. TV milestones)
Includes bibliographical references and index.
ISBN 0-8143-3082-7 (pbk. : alk. paper)
1. Rifleman (Television program) I. Title. II. Series.
PN1992.77.R528S53 2006
791.45'72—dc22

2005016950

∞ The paper used in this publication meets the minimum requirements of the
American National Standard for Information Sciences—Permanence of Paper for
Printed Library Materials, ANSI Z39.48-1984.

For Victor A. Sharrett
1905–1997

CONTENTS

ACKNOWLEDGMENTS

I extend limitless appreciation to Johnny Crawford for sharing with me his many memories of *The Rifleman* and early television. Robert Culp was similarly kind and generous for discussing with me his memories of his friend Sam Peckinpah, Culp's work on *The Rifleman*, his own TV western *Trackdown*, and numerous reflections on film and television.

I was especially fortunate to interview Arnold Laven, a director of *The Rifleman* and coproducer of the show with Levy-Gardner-Laven Productions; he remains vital in preserving the show's memory and contribution to television. He was exceptionally generous with his time and indulgent of my endless questions.

I am so very grateful to Barry Grant for his warm friendship and invaluable assistance in this project. Thanks also to Jeannette Sloniowski for her commitment to TV Milestones and this monograph. Annie Martin of Wayne State University Press is a most insightful and supportive editor. Jane Hoehner, the head of Wayne State University Press, was extraordinarily helpful to me.

I so enjoy conversations with Bill Luhr about the West, the western, and western culture. Krin Gabbard enlightens me all the time, pointing out my illogic and staying a good compañero. Sidney Gottlieb is a friend who helps me on fronts too numerous for me to make an adequate accounting. Joan Mellen and I comfort each other regularly about our respective projects. Mikita Brottman and David Sterritt are intellectual comrades who have added important thoughts to this writing. Pamela Grace is a terrific friend and colleague with wonderfully acute perceptions of mass culture. Heather Hendershot is another friend whose ideas have influenced this writing.

Arabella Rung was a dependable research assistant. Kathleen S. Dodds and Alan Delozier of the Seton Hall University archives provided material on the academic and athletic careers of Chuck Connors, who attended Seton Hall in the early 1940s.

David Curtis, Elaine Davis, Virginia Zic, Rosemary Greene, Spiros Antoniadis, and Nicole Cauvin are always wonderful, thoughtful friends. Larry Greene, who runs Seton Hall University's Multicultural Program, is a special friend whose brilliant mind always amazes me—I hope my feeble assistances to him are at least a partial repayment. Jurgen Heinrichs has been a very kind friend and very helpful to my recent work. My colleagues at Seton Hall's Department of Communication are a source of support to me, along with good friends in other departments—Gisela Webb, Judith Stark, Phil Kayal, Forrest Pritchett, Bill Sales, Rev. Lawrence Frizzell, and many others among them. Anthony and Michael D'Onofrio helped me with stills, as did Ron Davis of Video Lab. Levy-Gardner-Laven and Jerry Ohlinger's Movie Materials were key sources of still photos.

Joan Hubbard, my wife, is crucial to my life and how I look at the world. Her comments on *The Rifleman* and the western created new enthusiasms and made me reconsider old ones. Her fine sensibility has become a central part of my critical practice.

Night of the Gunmen

The Context

1

The Rifleman is the most compelling of the TV westerns that appeared at the end of the 1950s, the period in which the genre dominated the networks. My assertion is based not just on memories and the show's preeminence in its time slot for most of its five-year run (1958–63) on ABC but on the fascinating contradictions central to the show and its production circumstances.

The story of *The Rifleman* is innovative in that it presents, with uncommon drama and poignancy, a single-parent family struggling for survival in 1880s New Mexico. The show's unusual portrayal of domestic life threatened both by a dangerous frontier and internal stresses make its distinctive moral vision atypically honest for its day. Yet the seriousness of its drama, which offers a vision of family life more intelligent and sensitive than the ludicrous sitcoms that pretended to represent 1950s domesticity, also contains the conservatism—represented in part by gun violence as a solution to most problems—that flowed from the culture of the Cold War. While *The Rifleman* was a springboard for auteur director Sam Peckinpah—one of the key poets of the American postwar action cinema, who collaborated in the series with a wealth of talented actors and writers—it also represents the conflicts encumbering television authorship during its period.

One associates the era of the TV western with television's "golden age," a term that needs examination, since many critics view the golden age as the period 1946 to 1955—before the heyday of the TV western. The golden age was characterized by the experimentation underwritten by single sponsors that produced the comedy, variety shows, and, especially, live drama, the genre for which the period is perhaps best remembered. By the mid-1950s what Michele Hilmes terms the "classic network system" began to take hold,[1] with the three major networks becoming far more interventionist in programming. This led to a shift in production from New York–based live drama to Hollywood-produced filmed series as the film industry, threatened by television, found a way to participate in the medium.

The trend toward filmed series became more pronounced with the "public relations crisis" of the late 1950s,[2] as critics became disenchanted with television, especially in the wake of the famous game show scandals. The ABC network, created by Paramount, was among those that set the terms for network oversight. ABC is associated not only with the rise of the filmed series but with the predominance of the TV western as a genre; the western's formulas and innate conservatism were commercially safe within the culture of the period.[3] Thus the western served both the ideological and financial interests of early commercial television. The attempt by television to gain legitimacy, especially in the wake of the game show scandals, resulted chiefly in more commercialism and more corporate control, marked by the burgeoning of the TV western, as series such as ABC's *Warner Brothers Presents* introduced rotating western series such as *Cheyenne* (1955–63) and *Sugarfoot* (1957–61).[4]

The Rifleman both embodied and resisted the changing production dynamics of the period. It was conceived in 1957 by Levy-Gardner-Laven Productions, the independent production company of Jules Levy, Arthur Gardner, and Arnold Laven, who shopped it to the acclaimed producer-director Dick Powell, who had already established a reputation in early television through his Four Star Productions and *Dick Powell Theater*. Powell eventually brought *The Rifleman* to ABC. The series therefore retained some of the independent authorship (within the confines of commercial television, to be sure) characteristic of the medium's earliest days but was also emblematic of the network and Hollywood control of entertainment that would come to dominate broadcast television.

creation of show

Speculation about the reasons for the phenomenal rise and quick demise of the TV western has been considerable. The genre's importance to television, and the rise of *The Rifleman* as one of its outstanding examples, may be understood within the television culture of the 1950s and the period's ideological framework.

3

hist of genre

It is something of a truism that the western is the most endemically American film genre, both in terms of its production history in the United States and its close association with the narrative of the conquest of the American frontier. The western's roots in the novels of James Fenimore Cooper, Bret Harte, and Francis Parkman; the paintings of Frederic Remington and Charles Russell; and countless dime novels and stage melodramas have been well documented and are visible in the pictorial compositions, dialogue, and character construction of many cinematic westerns. After important and instructive early experiments such as *The Great Train Robbery* (1903) and rather distinguished narrative beginnings in works such as John Ford's *The Iron Horse* (1924), the genre fell on hard times with the rise of the matinee serial, featuring "singing cowboys" like Gene Autry. Ford—the man who said, "I make Westerns"—retrieved the genre from its kiddie status with *Stagecoach* (1939).[5]

pd. of genre

With few exceptions, the genre would maintain a stalwart conservatism until revisionism, represented by such films as Ford's *The Searchers* (1956), began to counter the western's notion of self and Other, objective good and evil, and the essential rightness of the white conquest of the West. It hardly seems ironic that the western's vision of a white, male-dominated civilization created in the nineteenth-century wilderness would appeal to audiences in the 1950s, one of the most conservative decades of the twentieth century. As the chief purveyor of private fantasy in the insulated, quiescent culture of postwar America, television westerns would be the main conduit of Americans' expansive utopian dreams.[6]

When discussing the rise of television, I sometimes ask students to name the predominant action-adventure genre of the early years of the medium. While some guess accurately, many are bewildered to learn of the western's extraordinary hegemony, with more than thirty shows filling the evening viewing schedule by 1959.[7] Richard Slotkin notes that from 1957 to 1961, the "average audience share [for TV western series] varied between 32.5 and 36 percent, reflecting a phenomenal level of audience interest."[8] By 1965 only a few shows remained, as the western, both in cinema and television, faded from view except for the conventions that influenced other genres (e.g., the gunfighter motifs of *Star Wars*, 1977). While the demise of the western remains a topic of scholarly debate, its place within early television culture is not especially hard to evaluate. A key point is that television culture was framed by the Cold War, which pervaded the economic and political environment of the era.

faded by '65

Almost immediately after the Allied victory in World War II, the United States painted the Soviet Union and, later, Maoist China as unrelenting adversaries in the postwar age. A new sense of alarm during the Cold War justified both military expenditures and a conservative mass culture. As Senator Arthur Vandenberg told President Harry S. Truman: "You're going to have to scare the hell out of the people."[9]

Cold War propaganda, which quickly found its way into entertainment, had a dual function. First, it instilled in the public the idea that the United States was under siege, a notion brought to fever pitch by McCarthyism and other efforts to stifle dissent and destroy any vestige of the activist leftist culture of the 1930s in order to advance U.S. business interests.[10] Cold War propaganda also created, as Slotkin has noted, the notion that any nation attempting to counter the dominance of U.S. economic interests must be merely a puppet of Moscow, its citizens in need of the enlightenment of U.S. corporate media or the deployment of the beneficent "gunfighters" in the CIA.[11] Such a climate was advantageous to the burgeoning electronic media business.

eras conserv. tone, capitalist promo.

5

Crucial to both the Cold War and the rise of television was the focus by corporate culture on what Elizabeth Fones-Wolf terms "selling free enterprise," with corporations frantic to convince the public that capitalism had to be protected from those promoting progressivism. Business still viewed the New Deal and labor union successes of the 1930s as dangerous threats and used radio, television, and virtually all channels of information and entertainment as the battleground for a culture war waged by public relations and advertising agencies to promote a conformism focused on capitalism and consumerism.[12]

Thus the Cold War and the socially conservative culture of the period 1945–65 were the context in which the TV western flourished.[13] Although the TV western and *The Rifleman* were born during the Cold War, it would be a mistake to assume that they were little more than a vehicle for a bullying sales pitch. On the contrary, among the factors that make *The Rifleman* important is its often centrist vision and its adoption of a spirit of reasonableness both out of step and in sync with the spirit of its age.

The Western Comes to TV

The 1950s saw a new social conformism in full bloom, as a jingoistic worldview took hold in many film and television genres, including science fiction (the alien invasion films), crime (film noir–influenced works, with their sense of impending chaos and apocalypse), and the western, whose unquestioning morality seemed especially suited to the period.

genre
possibility

6

While any number of westerns have a revisionist complexion—that is, they cast doubt on the creation story of the American West—from rather early in the genre's history, and certainly during the 1940s and 1950s in such films as *Duel in the Sun* (1946), *Johnny Guitar* (1953), *The Searchers* (1956), and *Man of the West* (1958), classic conservatism remained the genre's dominant characteristic throughout the Cold War years. Its conservatism was marked by optimism, in the belief that the American experience of "civilizing" Native Americans was right and proper, that a garden was indeed constructed in the wilderness during the Old West of the nineteenth century, even if the price was at times a bit high.

tv
ideology

The television western affirmed that conservatism but with its own touches of revisionism. This revisionism had less to do with questioning the conquest of the frontier than with opening a discourse of reasonableness consonant with the ideology of corporate liberalism and its politics of persuasion and centrism, regarded by business as its best weapons during its relegitimation in the 1950s following the postwar economic slide.[14] The TV western may be the most remarkable embodiment of an ideology that espoused centrist level-headedness (and domestic virtues) against extremism when such strategies as co-optation were practical, after which the state would not hesitate to use the brute force always associated with its rule.[15]

At first glance, the TV western would seem to have many of the kiddie aspects that the genre picked up during the heyday of cinematic singing cowboys in the 1930s. Mention the TV western, and anyone vaguely knowledgeable of the form might think of such characters as the Lone Ranger, Roy Rogers, Hopalong Cassidy, or several other film-to-television crossover figures whose franchises cultivated a large youth following. Indeed, Hopalong Cassidy was the first cowboy to reach television in 1949.

possible Kid focus

But these Saturday morning children's shows were not part of the phenomenon of the 1950s TV westerns, most of which were scheduled for evening prime time and for a relatively mature audience while still courting the youth market—indeed, one difficulty of the genre was the scheduling of some shows in the "marginal hour" of 9 P.M. when grammar school children were hustled off to bed.

7

A quick glance at a late 1950s television schedule reveals a unique feature of the TV western early in the medium's history: because producers of westerns sought large audiences of adults, they targeted adults, but the prime commercial sponsors of westerns were toy makers hawking toys based on the shows. The TV western in no small measure accounted for the success of a number of toy companies, such as Mattel, Marx, Hubley, and Hartland Plastics, which peddled play sets of ranches, forts, and frontier towns. But the single most popular toy item (at least for boys) was the toy gun, which makes sense because every one of the numerous TV western heroes carried at least one firearm. (We might profit from further study of the ways in which these ubiquitous toy guns fed the always-burgeoning gun culture of U.S. society.[16]) The more important point here is that *The Rifleman* was created for an adult audience while sustaining a large child market, making this pivotal TV western a reflection of 1950s domestic values.

time on sched. vs comm.

When westerns came to television, the contradictions of the genre were transferred along with them. At the very heart of the western is the building and validation of white civilization in the wilderness. Yet Doc Boone's final, rather resigned line in *Stagecoach*—as he and Curly set free the Ringo Kid (John Wayne) and his love interest, the prostitute Dallas (Claire Trevor)—"Well, they're saved from the blessings of civilization"[17]—suggests a peculiar ambivalence, one evident throughout the genre and in *The Rifleman*.

ambivalence toward cult

Stagecoach is among those defining westerns, along with *Shane* (1953), *High Noon* (1952), and *The Searchers*, that express doubt about the civilizing process, in part because of its association with domesticity. While "settler" westerns like *Bend of the River* (1952) pay homage to the building of the white community, their fixation is the allure and the threat of the male gunfighter. *The Searchers* might be interpreted as a film concerned with furthering western expansion, but its real attraction is the anguish of the individual male loner. *High Noon* would seem to repudiate civilization entirely in favor of the individual valor of the gunfighter. *The Rifleman* is the TV western's quintessential example of the struggle between the romance of individualism and the need to affirm the centrism and political-social acquiescence represented by the domesticity of 1950s suburban America.[18]

8

TV westerns such as *Wagon Train* (NBC, 1957–62; ABC, 1963–65) were melodramas leavened with action derived from the John Ford tradition of showing the conquest of the American West and all its travails. In *Wagon Train* (the show was in part inspired by Ford's *Wagonmaster* [1950]), the trail boss, Major Seth Adams, first played by Ford mainstay Ward Bond, intervened in family and interpersonal disputes—along with Indian attacks and various shoot-outs—as he took his wagon train of settlers across the plains during the 1957–62 television seasons. *Wagon Train* was "adult" in playing down action in favor of melodrama and in offering moral lessons that cohered to the social complexion of the times. This "settler" western was also notable in its extolling of domestic virtues not usually associated with the main impulses of the genre.

The majority of TV westerns were of the "gunfighter" mold, the locus of which was *Gunsmoke* (CBS, 1955–75), a series that ran for an incredible twenty years on the CBS network. Although by the end of its fifth season the show was becoming repetitive and even a little self-parodical, the story of the battles of Marshal Matt Dillon (James Arness) to clean up Dodge City became a genre archetype, figured first in the show's famous opening credits: Dillon enters frame left, the camera behind him. He is facing a foe in the distant background. Suddenly, the camera cuts to an extreme low angle of Dillon as the dramatic "face-off" music quickens. Dillon quickly draws his revolver and fires as the title appears on the screen and the theme music fills the sound track. Critics argue that the show's roots are in *High Noon*, a popular gunfighter western of the period, to be sure, but one too ideologically eccentric to be seen as the forebear of *Gunsmoke*. The show's influences are fairly conventional and supremely conservative, located in countless stories of strong men armed, of town tamers on the order of Wyatt Earp.

dominant type in genre

The taming of towns by men fast with a Colt .45 is basic to the genre, both cinematic and televisual, but *Gunsmoke*'s real novelty might lie in its unquestioning support of civilization and democratic values, at least insofar as these uphold the mission of the peace officer. In so doing, *Gunsmoke* creates a "good family" (Marshal Dillon, girlfriend Kitty, deputy Festus, friend Doc) that opposes monstrous bad families, a concept derived from the Wyatt Earp–Ike Clanton stories.[19] The theme of good and bad families reappears in *The Rifleman*; paramount is the notion of the savage clan that represents the return of the repressed and threatens domestic, civilized values and patriarchal law. The good-bad family dialectic places the TV western close to the ideology of the sitcom in its idealized portrayal of the American family; the con-

genre's basic struggle

9

tribution of innovative TV westerns such as *The Rifleman* is the problematizing of family and community.

Kara Ann Marling notes that the booming postwar western, especially the gunfighter variety, represented simply an escape from the Organization Man hyperconformism of the 1950s and the triumph of repression, sexual and political, as corporate capitalism continued its ascendancy.[20] Against this backdrop the western became very much a "boys' adventure" fantasy, representing a nostalgia for not only the lost innocence of an earlier America but the pleasure of an unbridled id, enjoying all sorts of license—including barely concealed threats to sexual mores—in an open, lawless arena. William Burroughs's novel *The Place of Dead Roads* rethinks the genre purely as homoerotic boys' escapism, a case not difficult to make. The gun fetishism and sexual freedom of *The Place of Dead Roads* is explicit in regard to guns or implicit regarding sexuality in *Wanted: Dead or Alive* (CBS, 1958–61), *Have Gun, Will Travel* (CBS, 1957–63), *Trackdown* (CBS, 1957–59), *The Rebel* (ABC, 1959–61; NBC, 1962), *Tombstone Territory* (ABC, 1957–59), *Colt .45* (ABC, 1957–60), *Cheyenne* (ABC, 1955–63), *Bronco* (ABC, 1958–62), and a host of other TV westerns. The peripheral role of women in the genre, despite (or precisely because of) their venerated status, constantly gives the lie to the traditional notions of machismo that the genre seems to uphold with a staunchness far beyond that of any other male-oriented genre. The TV western, like all westerns, has such a powerful attraction for men that it is often identified as an exclusively male genre in its orientations and appeal. This is true for the same reason that Doc Boone and Curly spoke cynically of the "blessings of civilization": men yearn for *a way out*, even if the premises of the escape are highly contradictory.[21]

The synthesis of gunfighter and settler western doesn't come easy to the TV western and its central focus, the pleasures of nonconformism and adventure figured in the lone male on the plains. The totally "pure" settler western has an obvious but awkward place in the TV western, a rather melodramatic and strained form not especially well integrated into the rest of the genre, even as it enjoyed a number of enduring representations. *Bonanza* is without question the archetypal TV settler western, its longevity (NBC, 1959–73) topped only by its gunfighter rival *Gunsmoke*. While both series played out their essential ideas early in their respective runs, *Bonanza* was always the less satisfying by far, its affiliations as much with melodrama and situation comedy as with the western. The show's highly unlikely and awkward conceits—the patriarch, Ben Cartwright (Lorne Greene), defends his Ponderosa Ranch with the help of his three grown sons, whose mothers were Ben's three wives—never helped the show's credibility. Especially noticeable in its absence from *Bonanza* is any sense of what it might mean for a man to raise three sons in the wilderness, as the series eschews any portrayal of the humdrum, grinding nature of domestic life on the frontier.

The settler western doesn't seem to have nearly the appeal of the gunfighter western, but its position in the TV western is rather prominent, answering particular ideological interests of the 1950s that are visible within *The Searchers*, a pivotal film of the decade that leaves tensions between settlers and gunfighters unresolved.[22] Other important films have exposed this false dichotomy, including *Man of the West* and *Unforgiven* (1993). In both films the gunman is fully integrated within civilization but then is revealed as implicitly, then overtly, monstrous. Emanations of the idea appear in *The Rifleman*, in forms often fascinating yet necessarily restrained, given the limits of commercial television of the period.

The appeal of both the settler and gunfighter versions of the TV western may be the establishment of a male province in which the female is marginalized; Michele Hilmes has noted that both in *Bonanza* and the far superior *The Rifleman* the female has been erased, with the absence of the woman

settler vs gunfighter 👆

can't really synthesize

11

companion creating a better avenue of escape for the males—
young and old—who want freedom from a domesticity often
conflated with conformism.[23]

This escape from conformity through the fantasy of the
TV western would have limited utility as the nation con-
fronted its enormous social-political problems in the 1960s
and 1970s. Only one show during the long television hegemony of the western successfully fused the gunfighter and
settler westerns and the genre's vision of 1950s America in a
way problematical to the assumptions of all phases of the
western. That show was *The Rifleman*.

The Series

The Rifleman is important not only for its fusion of settler-
gunfighter narratives, with all that this fusion represents for
both its genre and time, but also as one of the most accomplished, thoughtful, and enduring TV westerns. The show
held steady in its time slot during its five-year run. At the end
of its first season in 1963, the show went into regular syndi-
cation. For a time in the 1980s the show was marketed to the
Christian Broadcasting Network, later called the Family
Channel, which seemed fixated on the genre's conservative
values. The show was finally pulled from most broadcast cir-
culation when Levy-Gardner-Laven arranged for its release to
the retail video market in 1993.

The Rifleman tells the story of Lucas McCain (Chuck
Connors), a widower who journeys to 1880s New Mexico
with his young son, Mark (Johnny Crawford). The first
episodes focus on Lucas and Mark as they establish their
home, a ranch near the town of North Fork. Law and order
initially is in the hands of an ineffectual and compromised
marshal (R. G. Armstrong), whose murder by desperadoes introduces the show's other key character, Micah Torrance (Paul
Fix), a once-renowned peace officer fallen into alcoholism
after being badly injured by an adversary.

Lucas plays a central role in Micah's rehabilitation and return to the role of town peacekeeper. Lucas's close relationship with Micah—indeed, Lucas's indispensability when the law needs to be enforced—is central to the show's concept of justice. Lucas towers over Micah (Connors was 6' 6"). Lucas acknowledges the marshal's authority, but it is apparent—indeed a subject of several episodes—that Micah would be fairly helpless without Lucas. The two-character construct is basic to the show's contradictions concerning the rule of law and the authority of the male, which it inherits from the film side of the genre but refines it within the confines of 1950s political culture. The show recognized the institutions of law but portrayed the authority of the armed charismatic male as central to the civilizing process.

Lucas's ranch is a centerpiece of *The Rifleman*. Built at the Morrison property near Calabasas, California, under the authority of Four Star Productions, the ranch essentially became a character in the show.[24] With each episode we see Lucas and Mark putting up fences, fixing a wagon wheel, tending sick cattle, plowing a field, and accomplishing more strictly domestic chores such as churning butter, washing clothes and dishes, or watering a flower bed that Lucas keeps in memory of his late wife. The show is truly unusual in presenting a westerner who is a single parent—one with solid domestic values.

Also basic to the show, however, is the emphasis placed on Lucas as a rancher, not a farmer or low-status worker. In various episodes throughout the series many of Lucas's enemies call him "sodbuster," a term clearly meant to anger him by suggesting that he is associated with a lower class of men than that to which he—and the audience—aspire, namely, the middle class or a rung or two above. When Mark is unclear or frightened about the future of the ranch, as in the two-part "The Wyoming Story," in which the boy fears that he and his father might have to become dirt farmers to survive, Lucas is

13

Chuck Connors as Lucas McCain in *The Rifleman*

quick to remind Mark that "we're ranchers, son." The regular repetition of "sodbuster" in the series also underlines a basic moral distinction: Lucas is on the side of civilization and solid—even deliberately quaint—middle-class values, not the various representations of an untamed unconscious that threaten his world. Constantly throwing the denigrating term into Lucas's face is meant to stress his dignity.

Probably even more crucial to *The Rifleman*'s longevity is the affection expressed between father and son, the sense that Lucas is concerned not only with "raising Mark right" but with showing him parental love. Many episodes conclude with a heartfelt father-son reunion after a harrowing separation, with Mark running down the road to greet his father's advancing horse, then jumping up into his father's arms. Lucas raises his son with a combination of affection and loving but firm object lessons. He is also reasonable with Mark, rarely showing anger except when Mark has been disobedient to the point that he endangers himself. In this, *The Rifleman* shows a sense of child rearing taken straight from Dr. Spock, the era's foremost authority on a gentler, less authoritarian mode of raising children, one certainly removed from any of the physical violence or emotional imprudence often accepted in earlier decades. Various scholars have paid attention to the role of this form of parenting in the new conformism of postwar America.[25] Here and elsewhere in the show's themes, the series contains tendencies basic to the conservative western and unique to the cultural context of its moment, one that embodied a rather dubious liberalism.

Lucas's temperance and his domestic role do not for a moment divert us from a central theme that is explicit in the show's title. He has a weapon that is fused to his identity as settler and gunfighter. Lucas owns a custom-made .44-40 Winchester lever-action rifle, the lever of which was enlarged into an outsized, semicircular loop to allow the tall Lucas to twirl the weapon like a handgun. A small screw inserted through the rifle's trigger guard trips the trigger, so that Lucas can fire it automatically as he snaps the lever action shut against the stock. The device turns the weapon into a virtual

15

machine gun, as demonstrated in the show's explosive opening credits, among the most dynamic of any television action-adventure show of the era.

The rifle was discovered by producer-director Arnold Laven and Chuck Connors at Stembridge's, the leading Holly-

Raising Mark right: Lucas (Chuck Connors) and Mark (Johnny Crawford)

wood prop supply house, noted for its stock of prop firearms that was much in demand during the western's heyday.[26] With its large loop lever, the rifle was identical to—and could have been the same—weapon carried by John Wayne's Ringo Kid in *Stagecoach*. Laven thought that the rifle needed a distinctive feature; a Stembridge technician suggested the modification that gave the rifle its machine-gun rapidity and the show the dramatic edge that Lucas McCain's gunfighter persona would enjoy throughout its run.

The show opens with a close shot of Connors's gloved hands holding the rifle with its butt pressed to his right thigh, his right hand quickly working the large lever to fire a rapid volley of eleven shots at an unseen enemy as the actor walks slowly down the main street of North Fork. The camera then pans upward as the main title appears, revealing Chuck Connors as he reloads the gun with cartridges from his shirt pocket while an announcer intones the show's title and the star's name.

Although Lucas and the show seem to project a sense of reasonableness, there is no missing the central attraction. In many episodes Lucas's rifle, and his incredible proficiency with it, resolve trouble. Many a crisis facing North Fork is resolved in a sudden thunderous burst from Lucas's Winchester, whose explosion often seems an extension of the rage—or at least moral outrage—of its owner, so well projected by Chuck Connors, whose performance is often extraordinary. At times the mere sound of Lucas twirling the rifle and cocking the trigger is enough to back off the bad guys—or at least make the viewer sit forward in anticipation. Lucas's rifle also has a clear talismanic aspect, giving the show itself the mythical aura notable in the most memorable westerns. When Lucas is separated from the rifle—as in the episodes "The Angry Gun" or "The Vaqueros"—he is clearly diminished. When he reclaims the rifle, his authority is underscored in ways far exceeding his extraordinary marksmanship.

The rifle of *The Rifleman* would seem to make the show recognizably generic: markedly fetishistic weaponry is basic to many TV westerns, with stylized guns meant to give their bearers certain moral qualities and eccentricities that have a long pedigree in folklore. But the rifle was, in fact, what distinguished the series from other TV westerns. Lucas's rifle is meant to characterize him as domestic man, as settler, not as free-ranging adventurer, despite his prowess.

Lucas notes on several occasions (the early episode "The Angry Gun" contains the most explicit remark) that he is a rancher working in open country and that he carries a rifle to "hunt animals, not kill men." In this, the rifle imparts to Lucas's son one of many moral lessons as a practical tool to protect the homestead and, when need be, the community at large, not as a signifier of crime, frivolity, or unfettered machismo. When Shane tells a nervous Marion that his revolver is merely a tool, the audience cannot avoid Shane's background, which, even considering his virtue, is tainted with the criminality of gunfighting. Lucas's Winchester allows its owner a closer link with the land and the population, his gun prowess associated ambiguously (or so the main narrative of the series asserts) with civilization. Thus the Winchester is the symbol that identifies *The Rifleman* as a settler-gunfighter western, a fusion of domestic values and the adventurism-authority of patriarchal law.

This fusion is peculiarly underscored and problematized by the homosocial nature of the series, its rather closed society of men that in part speaks to the western as male-centered escapism in a conformist culture. Although Lucas and Mark interacted with a large number of people throughout the show's run, and evidenced interest in North Fork with all its joys and woes (Lucas refers to it as "my town"—he is clearly its leading citizen), Lucas is in many respects not *of* the town. He is a man both very domestic and of larger concerns, which largely excludes interest in women. As the series developed,

The explosive opening titles

Lucas gained a quasi-romantic relationship with Millie Scott (Joan Taylor), an often teary-eyed storekeeper, and later with Lou Mallory (Patricia Blair), owner of the North Fork hotel. Yet neither of these relationships seemed authentic in the sense of providing Lucas with a "love interest." In part, the show appears to be concerned here with preserving Lucas as grieving widower, his dead wife the archetypal Madonna (she is portrayed explicitly as such in one episode—"The Vision"—seen by Mark in a fever dream as he lies deathly ill). Because the woman in his life is a memory, Lucas gains moral stature—he is a living testament to the virtue that she embodies. Or so the series sometimes suggests. (Clint Eastwood's *Unforgiven* deconstructs the image of the widower-rancher, suggesting that the ongoing tribute paid by the husband to his late wife is largely a lie and a facade that conceals roiling pathologies within, undercutting the notion of the female as the strongest "civilizing" force on the frontier.)

The most apparent dramatic function of Lucas's role as widower is to free him for adventure. Of course, the dead wife, and Lucas's refusal to replace her, adds poignancy, the element of melodrama so popular in 1950s culture. The father-son bonding, the many heartfelt returns of Lucas to his son, point to the loneliness and anxiety of domestic existence. The action-adventure "gunfighter motifs" of the series are meant to valorize this existence and support its basic goodness, but they often only underscore the boredom and inertia of day-to-day life. At its very worst, the absence of a woman from the domestic scene turns Lucas and Mark into an action team that threatens to evoke Batman and Robin, although the show never deserts its essential construct, one at the absolute core of male-oriented genre fiction: an older man passing knowledge of the male world to the next generation through his young acolyte.

The Rifleman presents us with many issues that make it important to the TV western—and the genre in general—of

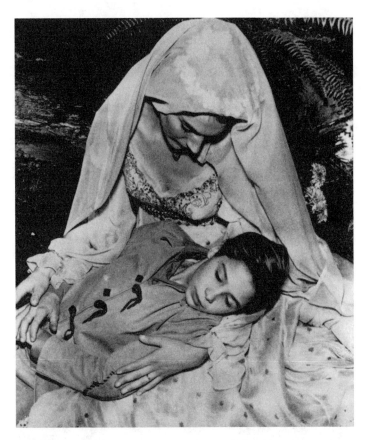

The female as Madonna: a stricken Mark dreams of his dead mother in "The Vision"

the late 1950s. The show has a strong sense of tolerance (many episodes dealt with racial injustice), forbearance, and reason, embodied in the stalwart, solid-citizen image of rancher Lucas McCain. On the other hand, the show relies on conventions basic to the gunfighter western, often in their most hyperbolic manifestation.

The seemingly contradictory vision of *The Rifleman* found its way into the aforementioned merchandizing of the day: a toy version of Lucas's "flip rifle," along with action figurines of Lucas McCain that played off of the show's "gunfighter" appeal, while lunch boxes and a "Rifleman Ranch" play set suggested the TV western's domestic virtues.[27] The play sets underscored the sense of the TV western's "safeness" and a form of escapism that would encourage domestic values, while toy guns foster traditional masculinity.[28] These features, it must be said, raise further critical issues for future investigation, because the show's producers focused solely on *The Rifleman*, with the merchandizing left to other entrepreneurs, who would consult with and pay the producers after the series was launched.[29]

The contradictions of the show don't render it incoherent, nor are they unusual in the attempt to create within the era's dominant culture a sense of reasonableness while also promoting conformism, the enforcement of which is not afraid of the resort to violence. What is noteworthy about *The Rifleman* is its sense of authenticity as it struggles with an out-

Television offers a world in miniature: The toy *Rifleman* play set

look full of conflict—the extolling of progressive values even as it presents the issue most central to the western, the man-boy relationship, and the preservation of masculine values in the United States.

Origins

The creation of *The Rifleman* was an example of Hollywood film and television production as both collaborative arts and auteurism, because the legendary director Sam Peckinpah was central to the show's inception and early episodes, and his imprint was evident long after he left the series.

The title of the show was conceived by coproducer Jules Levy years before the team of Levy-Gardner-Laven had a concept for the show, much less a script.[1] Although single authorship in a medium such as television is a rarity, the writing of Sam Peckinpah was central to the show.[2] And in saying this I am not replacing Peckinpah, the writer-director who changed the face of the western as it entered its revisionist phase, with "Peckinpah," a deconstructionist conceit that assumes the man is no more than a vague sum of ideological effects or that his works must be read apart from the person who created them. Peckinpah was a product of his age but a creative one, whose work embodied (and resisted) the ideological imperatives of the postwar period. The vision in *The Rifleman* can best be understood by setting it against Peckinpah's other work.

Peckinpah's themes in *The Rifleman* recur in such films as *Ride the High Country* (1962), *The Wild Bunch* (1969), *The Ballad of Cable Hogue* (1970), *Junior Bonner* (1972), *Pat Garrett and Billy the Kid* (1973)—virtually all his major and minor films. Peckinpah wrote for a number of TV westerns in the late 1950s, including *Gunsmoke*; *Have Gun, Will Travel*; *Trackdown*; *Tombstone Territory*; *Johnny Ringo* (CBS, 1959–60); *Broken Arrow* (ABC, 1956–60); and *Tales of Wells Fargo* (NBC, 1957–62). One need not read the closing credits to ascertain Peckinpah's creative affiliation with a given episode, and never was this more true than with *The Rifleman*. Peckinpah's presence complicates the narratives and ideological ambitions of the show.

Peckinpah's work on *The Rifleman* occurred as he suffered one of many stings in Hollywood, in this instance a falling-out with Marlon Brando over a script that Peckinpah had written from a novel by Charles Neider called *The Authentic Death of Hendry Jones*; the script eventually became the film *One-Eyed Jacks* (1960), a cryptic, Oedipal retelling of the Billy the Kid story that was to have been directed by Stanley Kubrick. (The story would get Peckinpah's full attention more than fifteen years later in *Pat Garrett and Billy the Kid*.) *One-Eyed Jacks* tells the story of Kid Rio, a bank robber, and his mentor, Dad Longworth (the Oedipal material is almost laughably recognizable). Peckinpah's script had little relation to the final film, which Brando himself lyrically directed after Kubrick was fired. Stories of fathers (or father figures) and their sons are a powerful feature of Peckinpah's work; some of what he scrapped in *One-Eyed Jacks* he used in *The Rifleman*.

The Rifleman began as a script that Peckinpah shopped to freelance producers Jules Levy, Arthur Gardner, and Arnold Laven. Laven, himself a seasoned director, would be a prominent creative force in the show, directing key episodes, including the pilot, "The Sharpshooter," and "Home Ranch," both Peckinpah scripts that Laven directed with remarkable sensitivity. Levy and Gardner would guide the show's financing and production in conjunction with Dick Powell. Laven had worked with Peckinpah when the Levy-Gardner-Laven team developed a story about Custer's Last Stand based on a novel called *The Dice of God* by Hoffman Bitney.[3] Although the project fizzled (it would be resurrected as *The Glory Guys*, a 1965 film directed by Laven), Laven was impressed with Peckinpah as a person and writer, and the two quickly developed a cordial relationship.[4] Peckinpah brought Laven a telescript that would be crucial to his career. It was called "The Sharpshooter," about a wandering gunman who enters a small-town shooting contest. Although he is clearly the expert shot in the competition, the brutal local land baron makes the gunman throw the match and leave town humiliated. As Peckinpah presented "The Sharpshooter" to Levy-Gardner-Laven initially, it appears to have been a sketch dealing with Peckinpah's recurrent theme of lost or compromised ideals, one that gained currency in the 1950s phase of the psychological-political western that began with *High Noon*. Laven suggested adding a boy, the sharpshooter's son, who would be threatened by the local thugs, giving the sharpshooter more dignity in his defeat.[5] Peckinpah responded positively, adding the change and fleshing out the story.

Soon the William Morris Agency, which represented the producer, showed the Levy-Gardner-Laven project to actor-director Dick Powell; Powell, Ida Lupino, Charles Boyer, and David Niven owned an independent production company called Four Star Productions. Four Star was a credible artistic force in early television, creating *Four Star Playhouse* and *Dick Powell's Zane Grey Theater* (CBS, 1956–62), both anthology series showcasing, in the manner of the distinguished *Playhouse 90* (CBS, 1956–61), some formidable writing, directing, and acting talent before the crackdown that would give increasing authority to networks and Hollywood studios. Powell presented the script to Tom MacDermott of the powerhouse advertising firm of Benton and Bowles—as David Weddle noted, the show was produced at the tail end of the golden age, when advertisers, rather than the networks, played the key role in determining television programming.[6] "The Sharpshooter" appeared on *Zane Grey Theater*; it would be the beginning of *The Rifleman*. When Proctor and Gamble and Ralston-Purina agreed to sponsor the show, *The Rifleman* entered the fall 1958 schedule.[7]

The Rifleman had a number of important creative mainstays, including directors such as Laven, Ted Post, Tom Gries, Ida Lupino, Richard Donner, and Arthur Hiller, people who directed some of the most compelling episodes. Joseph H. Lewis, the ingenious director of *Gun Crazy* (1950) and *The Big Combo* (1955), would become "house director"[8]; after Peckinpah and Laven, Lewis would be most responsible for *The Rifleman's* emotionally complicated edge. A figure key to the identity of the show was the composer Hershel Burke Gilbert, who created *The Rifleman's* memorable main theme and score. The lilting, ballad-like theme, one of the most memorable for TV westerns, often formed motifs in the series, becoming a percussion-enhanced, clip-clopping signal of happiness, return, and reunion or a dark, brooding, string-driven portent of danger.

David Weddle has noted that much of the content of the early episodes of *The Rifleman* came from Sam Peckinpah's origins and personal history. The town of North Fork and the valley where Lucas and Mark establish their ranch are references to Peckinpah's boyhood in rural California. Weddle notes that the dialogue of the episodes that Peckinpah wrote or directed have moments that evoke his famous acerbic wit, as when, in "The Marshal," a devious killer (James Drury) tells a seemingly outgunned Micah Torrance: "You'll have to get a lot closer to make that scattergun pay for its freight," or, as two hoodlums stagger into the town saloon, one tells the other, "I ain't gonna ruin a ten-dollar drunk with a two-bit meal!"[9]

Although many talented actors began in early television, *The Rifleman* is notable for a stock company of villains and supporting players who would be associated with Peckinpah and some of the better-known westerns and action films of the 1950s, 1960s, and 1970s. Especially prominent are Warren Oates, Lee Van Cleef, Robert Wilke, Denver Pyle, Robert Culp (a close friend of Peckinpah's), James Coburn, Jack Elam, Robert Webber, John Dehner, Vic Morrow, Dennis Hopper, R. G. Armstrong, Royal Dano, James Drury, Michael Ansara, and Sammy Davis, Jr., whose prowess with guns earned him slots in two episodes (he was reported to have been on an early list for the cast of *The Wild Bunch*). The villainy and violence that these actors brought to *The Rifleman* was not typical of the genre as a whole. The evil of the show's villains, especially in its early seasons, suggests a savagery and amorality foreshadowing the revisionist phase of the western. Not surprisingly, the show was among the more violent TV westerns, its gunplay slipping past censors because much of the action is centered ultimately on moral lessons, a device that justified a great deal of violence in television action-adventure shows of the period. Episodes of *The Rifleman* often contain prolonged treachery or sadism—against Lucas, Mark, Micah, or an innocent of the town—culminating in an explosion of Lucas's rifle fury, a dramatic structure that would show up in Peckinpah's films.

The moral universe of the series became complicated as aspects of Lucas's limitations developed, including a racial bigotry that was tempered by Lucas's sense of "fairness." The racial and gender assumptions underlying this and most television programs are challenged primarily in the show's gradual confrontation with its hero. As portrayed by Chuck Connors, a hulking yet lithe former athlete whose stint with the Brooklyn Dodgers was central to his early publicity, Lucas McCain is a hero whose incipient monstrousness lurks close to the surface, a notion developed in one of the best episodes,

"The Deadly Image," wherein Lucas confronts a terrible doppelganger.

Johnny Crawford, the son of a talented musical family and a veteran (at age ten) of Disney's *Mickey Mouse Club* (1955–56), was cast in the role of Mark McCain. Crawford's interaction with Connors is often extraordinary in its instincts and intelligence, only occasionally capitulating to directorial demands for the cloying gestures often asked of child actors. Crawford's innocence is counterbalanced by a canny understanding of the world around him, including his father's darker nature, an idea crucial to the series.

Sam Peckinpah left *The Rifleman* in the first season, returning occasionally for some of its more distinctive moments, including "The Boarding House," an episode that contains Peckinpah's peculiar mixture of tolerance, romanticism, and reaction. Peckinpah apparently wanted the series to focus on Mark, so that the series would be a kind of bildungsroman, showing, in Peckinpah's words, Mark's discovery of "what it's all about."[10] Peckinpah was referring, no doubt, to his sometimes essentialist, reductionist view of a violent world, one beset by the vile appetites of a new technocracy that was opposed by the hopelessly compromised yet relatively moral few. Such a vision would find its way, probably in a more refined form than he conceived at the time, into his best films (*Ride the High Country, The Wild Bunch, Junior Bonner, Pat Garrett and Billy the Kid*) but was not acceptable in any form to 1950s commercial television. For one thing, the series would have been something of a miniseries, a short novel showing Mark's growth, maturation, possible disillusionment. *The Rifleman* indeed dealt with Mark's growing up: Johnny Crawford's becoming a teenager damaged the heart-warming appeal built into the show's many vignettes of father-son bonding, reunion, and mutual affection, images more appealing when Crawford was still a little boy. But rather than show a consistent series of bitter trials from Mark's point of view, the show's stories often were constructed as lessons in growing up. Arnold Laven recalls that Peckinpah's departure from the show was based less on philosophical differences than on Peckinpah's insistence on a level of violence that the producers felt distasteful and unsuited to their concept.[11]

Despite the disappointment that Peckinpah felt with the direction of *The Rifleman*, he would develop another TV western with Dick Powell that ran for one half-season (thirteen episodes) on NBC in 1960. Titled *The Westerner* and starring Brian Keith, the show is probably the most radical TV western ever produced, reflecting fully Peckinpah's gritty directorial sensibility. The show so displeased the network and sponsor that it occupies a unique place in television history—when it aired, it was canceled in the first ten minutes of the first episode.[12] Yet long after Peckinpah's departure, *The Rifleman* would retain features associated with his artistry and the sensibility that he brought to the western, including a pervasive sense of melancholy and an often savage violence, associated as much with the fury and narrowness of the hero and the community that he represents as with the often bestial others who function as interlopers, destroyers of a normality that is often deceptive.

The Domestic Frontiersman
and the Vital Center

While many TV westerns of the 1950s encapsulated the tendency toward a sense of moderation, centrism, and civility, with recourse to violence always at the ready, *The Rifleman* remains the key exemplar. The western loner has long been characterized as a watchful, slow-to-react man whose wisdom complements his physical skills, but Chuck Connors's Lucas McCain reconfigures the westerner very much as an embodiment of 1950s culture.

McCain contains all the values of the 1950s domesticated man inasmuch as he attempts to persuade, is open to persuasion, and raises his son in an atmosphere that extols reason, level-headed practicality, and no-nonsense hard work. McCain is also the enforcer of the status quo, the show's message of tolerance and forbearance always circumscribed by the ideological assumptions of the era that understood armed force as a necessary—and not always last—resort.

Thus the political context of the 1950s is key to understanding the themes of *The Rifleman*. Cold war and corporate liberals, represented most famously by Arthur Schlesinger, Jr., and his concept of the "vital center," argued against extremist ideologies of the left and right (their real concern, of course, was the former), considering the U.S. political landscape best served when the ideological pendulum remained in the center.[1] Wary of soft-headed emotionalism, Schlesinger remarked that "sentimentality has softened up the progressive for Communist permeation and conquest."[2]

Cold War liberalism and the values of domestic centrism even found their way into one of the most popular television westerns and mass culture fads of the decade: the Davy Crockett episodes of Walt Disney's *Disneyland* show, created in part to promote Disney's new theme park in Anaheim.[3] Fabled "Indian fighter" Davy Crockett (Fess Parker) begins two key episodes at home with his wife, Polly, and their "young 'uns," although he is inevitably summoned off to battle. Parker's Crockett is a fair-minded older brother, never belligerent, always wanting to settle things with a friendly chat seasoned with humorous, self-deprecating tall tales. For Crockett and McCain, violence is a last resort. Like McCain, Crockett's hand is out to his Indian rivals, and his opposition to racial bigots is fiery, a portrayal reasonably close to the historical Crockett.[4] This ultimate boys' hero of 1950s television contains not an ounce of swagger, particularly when we get to "Davy Crockett Goes to Congress," a tale of a plainspoken, full-of-fun backwoods spokesman for the common man. Like Lucas McCain, Disney's Crockett becomes a widower, bearing his grief hard but with fewer responsibilities than Lucas, underscoring the notion of the female as ennobled in death, allowing the male to continue with the crucial project of frontier adventure while enjoying his personal freedom. Yet for all his humor, love of home, and low-key affability, Crockett's stories are about his vanquishing of adversaries and his sacrificial death at the Alamo—in other words, the professionalism and commitment to armed force that McCain also embodied. While Disney's Crockett is the enduring icon of the 1950s, Lucas McCain offers significant inflections on themes in the Crockett stories, especially through the emphasis on male domesticity.

The Professional

The more generic conventions of *The Rifleman* focus not on Lucas the rancher but on Lucas the symbol of male professionalism, the man adept with guns and male judgment. In so doing, the series emphasized early in its run traditional and conservative qualities of the male frontiersman that protect domestic values. The pilot episode is titled, after all, "The Sharpshooter." The episode introduced Lucas's extraordinary skills as a marksman as he enters a turkey shoot to win some money for a down payment on the new ranch. Lucas is intimidated into throwing the match by the town bully and crime boss (Leif Erickson), who threatens to kill Mark if Lucas does not comply, setting up a central dilemma of many episodes—Mark is Lucas's vulnerability, the promise of the continuation of his name and male authority in the frontier community. The title of the episode is a bit ambiguous, because Lucas competes with a hair-trigger Billy the Kid type (a very young Dennis Hopper just after his roles in *Rebel Without a Cause* [1955] and *Giant* [1956]) whose heart isn't in his work; the Hopper character is bullied by a belligerent uncle who exploits the young man's talent. This sets up another of the show's basic themes: the terrible parent versus the sober and loving Lucas, a notion that would become problematized as the series evolved. After the uncle is murdered by local hoodlums in the employ of the boss, Lucas clears up the problems of the young gunfighter and brings low the hoodlums themselves, winning the money to establish his ranch and setting North Fork on the path toward civilization.

The episode "The Angry Gun" introduces some archetypal "journey" themes of the western, including ideas refined

Lucas defends North Fork with help from a young gunfighter (Dennis Hopper) in "The Sharpshooter"

by the films of Anthony Mann that involve an arduous trek that is in fact a trial of character. In "The Angry Gun" Lucas confronts the first in a line of sadistic psychopaths, the bandit Johnny Cotton (Vic Morrow). Cotton is being transported under custody to the territorial prison on the stagecoach that is carrying Lucas and Mark home from a cattle auction. Cotton salivates over the "fine lever-action rifle," and a discourse commences about the virtues of a revolver over a rifle. It is in this episode that Lucas explains that he is a rancher, that he uses his gun to "hunt animals, not kill men." Cotton scoffs at Lucas; Cotton's advocacy of the revolver serves to underscore his villainy, his place outside the domestic order. Cotton's gang holds up the stage, shoots the sheriff guarding Cotton, and makes off with Lucas's money and his rifle. Despite Cotton's earlier disdain for rifles, he obviously sees a certain totemic quality in Lucas's extraordinary weapon, as if Cotton wants to absorb the superior man's charisma by stealing it. Lucas sends Mark home and sets out after the bandits on foot, figuring "they'll be leading their animals more than riding them over this rough country." Lucas traverses hilly, parched terrain, beleaguered as much by Cotton's psychotic taunts as by the physical ordeal. Eventually, the two men square off, Lucas with a scavenged revolver, Cotton firing randomly at Lucas with the stolen rifle, Cotton shouting taunts as he shoots, reminding Lucas of the range and power of his own weapon. Lucas meanwhile turns his scrap revolver into a rifle by rigging a piece of board as a stock and a twig as a rear sight. He kills a bewildered Cotton with two quick shots. The dying Cotton hands Lucas his rifle. Lucas, with typically gentle paternalism, touches the head of the youthful outlaw. The obvious lesson is that Lucas's superiority does not come from weapons alone, or even his special understanding of them, but from his goodness, endurance, and moral superiority, each attribute reinforcing the others. Lucas's rifle is clearly established as his Excalibur, a sacred object whose power will be realized only in righteous hands. Lucas's frightening journey over barren hills, then back to the embrace of his son at the fertile McCain ranch, is a journey of psychological crisis—underscored by the encounter with the demented Johnny Cotton—that ends in the restoration of domestic wholeness.

In "The Marshal," probably the most important Peckinpah episode, Lucas comes upon Micah Torrance, a famed lawman severely injured long ago, now fallen into alcoholism and self-deprecation. The episode takes the view that alcoholism and similar illnesses are failures of character, a view always much favored by conservatism. Lucas helps Micah recover a lost sense of self by putting him to work on the McCain ranch and forcing him to quit whining about past failures. During the episode three bandits (James Drury, Warren Oates, Robert Wilke) arrive in North Fork to exact revenge on Micah for arresting them years earlier. They discover his infirmities and decide to wreck and rob the town. One bandit, a stranger to Lucas, attempts to befriend him and thereby lure him into town, recognizing that he is the only force capable of preventing the chaos that the three bandits want to unleash. Lucas tells Micah of his encounter with the seemingly benevolent stranger as he saddles his horse to ride into town. Micah admonishes Lucas that he is being suckered by a man with "an easy way." Lucas ignores Micah and rides into an ambush. Fortunately, Micah screws up his courage, throws off the last fog of alcohol, and rides into town in time to rescue Lucas and finish off the bandits with a shotgun, a weapon that would become Micah's trademark, the devastating gun of a man who can no longer shoot straight.

The episode's point is clear: Micah's age and infirmities are really emblems of his experience and judgment. While Lucas is strong and courageous, Micah is wise. The episode is basic Peckinpah in its image of the aging westerner, his scars, failed dreams, and essential dignity in the face of a changing landscape. It is also an archetypal western in its valorization of the older man as teacher to the younger one, an idea fundamental to the series but embodied here not in Lucas's instructions to Mark but in Lucas's lessons from Micah. Unfortunately, the Lucas-Micah relationship did not retain much of this dynamic throughout the show's run. While Micah is allowed his dignity and occasional moments of indispensability, his authority in North Fork seems peripheral to the huge physical and moral presence of Lucas (Micah's acute awareness of the problem is exploited to some dramatic effect in a few episodes). Numerous episodes make the point, including "The Deadly Wait," in which Lucas, although severely wounded by a sadistic killer (Lee Van Cleef) who is terrorizing Micah because of an old grievance, struggles from his sick bed with Herculean effort and rescues Micah in the nick of time.

Questions of the role of the law are developed further in "The Letter of the Law." Micah takes into custody a psychopathic gunman named Stocker (Vic Morrow). Micah deputizes Lucas because he is worried that Stocker's friends might descend on the town. Descend they do, kidnapping Micah and holding him hostage until Lucas releases Stocker. Lucas agonizes over the dilemma, finally freeing Stocker to gain Micah's release. Micah has in the meantime fled his captors and is wounded in the process. When he returns to North Fork, Micah is angry at Lucas for not following the letter of the law. Lucas, as it develops, has a plan to recapture Stocker. In releasing the outlaw Lucas forced him to leave behind his prized custom-made revolvers, aware that the outlaw will return for the heavily fetishized weapons. Lucas is right, and he guns down Stocker and his pals when they return to the marshal's office at night to retrieve the pistols. Lucas and Micah have a minor tiff over Lucas's placing his affection for Micah ahead of the law, but by the epilogue all is well. The lesson here is less about the rigidity of the law and the demands of the heart than about showing Lucas to be a fully developed person, his instincts and inherent righteousness once again marking him, not the man wearing the badge, as the true male professional. The domesticated citizen within Lucas takes a backseat to his masculine judgment.

The acuity of Lucas's instincts comes into play in "The Man from Salinas," wherein a cunning bounty hunter (Robert Culp in a fine, quirky performance) comes to North Fork to retrieve the body of a dead outlaw on the pretext that he is the

Facing down a psycho (Lee Van Cleef) in "The Deadly Wait"

outlaw's brother. From the outset Lucas senses something is awry in the bounty hunter's smarmy, overly solicitous nature, even as the rest of the gullible townspeople seem impressed

The real law: Micah deputizes Lucas

with the man's apparently sincere grief. Lucas does some detective work and learns that the dead outlaw had no family. Lucas faces off against the bounty hunter in one of the show's innumerable street showdowns. In this situation, as in many episodes, Lucas's expression that "something wasn't right" refers to an interloper's violating the norms of his town.

The protection of normality often takes instructive forms in regard to the concept of civilization that Lucas and North Fork stand for. In "The Money Gun" a professional killer named King (John Dehner) is hired by an irate citizen to kill Oat Jackford (Bert Freed), a megalomaniacal rancher whose spread borders Lucas's. Lucas and Jackford had crossed paths in the second episode, "Home Ranch" (written by Peckinpah), in which Jackford tries to buy Lucas out (Lucas responds with typical Peckinpah: "You couldn't buy it for money, marbles, or chalk"), just after one of Jackford's gunmen decides to burn Lucas's house. Jackford is outraged on hearing of the destruction but nevertheless demands that Lucas move on, because his ranch is blocking Jackford's plans to expand his control of the local cattle business (shades of *Shane*). After a tussle to prove who is bull of the woods, Jackford and Lucas shake hands, with Jackford agreeing to rebuild Lucas's ranch.

In many respects "Home Ranch" is the most telling representation in the series of the spirit of corporate liberalism. Oat Jackford is not Rufe Ryker of *Shane*, much less Frank Stanton of *Heaven's Gate* (1980). Jackford's patently monopolistic impulses do not conflict with the show's sense that "there's room here for everybody," as it regularly features Jackford as a tough-minded and ornery but solid citizen. In "The Money Gun" Jackford reveals the professional assassin King to be a spineless cur, with Jackford himself beating King nearly to death. King's evil is outweighed, however, by the local who hired him, who shoots the badly beaten King, only to be arrested by Lucas and Micah. Jackford's bullying and economic authority over the community, though a nuisance, are outweighed by the personal depravity of King and the more depraved local who hired him.

Jackford, like Lucas, is a symbol, if in Jackford's case a not appealing one, of the necessary expansionist project and domestication of the frontier. King is nothing more than a barbaric throwback—like many of the western's knight-errant gunfighters—and the corporate liberal–middle-class values of *The Rifleman* seldom romanticize the free spirit of the gunman. This spirit is emphasized by King's former role as a lawman, during which he had a professional relationship with Lucas. As might be imagined, Lucas was the good lawman and King the bad; King was not terribly interested in whether the culprits he arrested were brought in dead or alive.

Yet the encounter with King is important, because it brings up a notion that the series would develop, at times with a degree of hyperbole. While *The Rifleman* tends to remove from the hero any sense of the moral ambiguity that we see in the hero of *Shane*, the notion of Lucas's having a dark side becomes a recurring theme, one that arose in the genre as it evolved in the 1960s. Lucas's past—one that seems to have its dark moments but is otherwise wholesome—receives little real exposition. His history, like that of the postwar Organization Man, seems irrelevant, because only the present of renewed commitment to domestic civilization—not rumination over the miserable awakenings of a past life—is relevant. This basic trajectory is undercut, however, as the show eventually focuses on the latent savagery of its hero, leaving to our imaginations the full details of his early life, which are partially sketched in some episodes that I discuss in this chapter.

The Civilizing Force

As I have suggested, *The Rifleman* gains its principal distinction from its argument in favor of domestic life, the love of a father for his son, and the advocacy, however disingenuous, of reasoned persuasion over brute force. Lucas McCain's construction as the embodiment of these virtues takes on grand and banal forms, suggesting at points that Lucas is the quintessential emblem of westward expansion, the embodiment of fair play and reason, even if he needs to enforce them with a rifle. At other points he is an emblem of common sense, a virtue whose deceptive simplicity is portrayed as central to democracy. Throughout the show's run, *The Rifleman* was adept at keeping these qualities in plausible balance.

In the early episode "The Sheridan Story," Lucas, a Union veteran of the Civil War, becomes another of the western's symbols of the war's centrality to nineteenth-century America (this important and recurrent backstory is rather undeveloped, perhaps because the extreme divisiveness symbolized by the Civil War runs against the show's centrism). In *The Rifleman*, as in many movie and TV westerns of the era, the Civil War was not yet portrayed as a catastrophe with devastating consequences for the United States, as it would be in *Shenandoah* (1965) and *The Outlaw Josey Wales* (1976). In "The Sheridan Story" Lucas reenacts the forging of the Union when he takes in a wandering and impaired Confederate veteran, Frank Blandon (Royal Dano in one of his best television roles). Feeling kinship with and sympathy for an old man severely down on his luck, Lucas puts Blandon to work on the ranch. After Blandon suffers a freak accident, Mark notices the terrible, poorly healed injuries of the old Johnny Reb. The scene provides one of the show's poignant moments of father-son consolation, as Lucas regrets that he cannot protect Mark from the woes of life.

Shortly afterward a patrol of federal troops arrives at the McCain ranch led by Gen. Phil Sheridan (Lawrence Dobkin), who is on an inspection tour as "military governor of the southwest territories." He recognizes Lucas McCain as one of his former officers; Lucas is happily surprised, then troubled by the general's presence. The McCain ranch soon becomes another Appomattox Court House, the site of Robert E. Lee's surrender. Blandon is at first outraged by Sheridan's presence on the ranch and plans to assassinate him, until Sheridan's feeling of comradeship for the vanquished Rebel stirs Blandon's emotions. The episode concludes with Sheridan planning to take Blandon east for proper treatment of his war injuries, following Lincoln's admonition to the federal forces to "bind up the nation's wounds."

The Rifleman is far too intelligent to repeat yet another Hollywood romanticization of the lost cause of the Confederacy in the manner of most productions dealing with the Civil War. Rather, it presents the war as a prelude to the civilizing process that took root in the West and offers the benign, bucolic face of this process rather than the industrialized hell of wage slavery and the limits of Reconstruction. Above all, the episode is about a meeting of minds, a reconciliation of ideological extremes that is the perfect emblem of the show's version of corporate liberalism. Significantly, it presents Lucas as crucial to the healing of postbellum America, as this key episode establishes him as competent male whose skills were tested in war and as a civil man who mediates disputes and effectuates social healing. "The Sheridan Story," written by the veteran Cyril Hume, appeared midway in the show's first season and is a key example of its significance and intelligence (less than two years earlier Hume had written, with Nicholas Ray, an extraordinary meditation on 1950s culture, *Bigger Than Life* [1956]).

In "End of a Young Gun," another early and defining episode, Lucas offers a disaffected young outlaw (Michael Landon) some simple instruction in the virtues of domestic (what Lucas calls "regular") life. The outlaw comes to the McCain ranch after rescuing Mark from a fall, showing the outlaw character's basic humanity and availability to domestication, especially as he falls in love with a local girl while recovering from injuries sustained while helping Mark. At one point the outlaw watches Lucas fix a wagon wheel. Lucas kneels near his work, bare-chested and perspiring in the hot sun, as he removes the wheel and greases the axle, exemplifying the dignity of hard work. The outlaw complains that a wealthy man stole the ranch that his own family once had. Lucas gives the young outlaw a dressing-down, suggesting that he is crying over spilled milk instead of looking to the future and opportunity, arguing that "there are a dozen ranches around here—none of them were stolen" and suggesting that what happened to the young man's family is an aberration. At the episode's end the young outlaw's gang returns to retrieve him; the outlaw refuses to leave, and Lucas intervenes, shooting down the bandits and removing from the young hoodlum any further arguments against domesticity. In the epilogue the young outlaw promises to return stolen money and to return to the sweetheart he met at the McCain ranch. Lucas concludes the episode with remarks to his son about the incipient goodness in all men.

In "The Schoolmaster" Lucas takes on the role of mediator of frontier values, that is, the "common sense" and anti-intellectual stance of the middle class, and the building of civilization. Mark has difficulties with the new schoolmaster of the town, Griswold (Arnold Moss), a character just a hair removed from Dickens's monstrous overseers of children. As the episode opens, Lucas takes a number of local children to school in his buckboard wagon—among his numerous civic roles, he is the school bus driver. Griswold is perturbed that Lucas is late with the children, doubly angry when he sees Lucas's rifle, arguing that guns have no place around children. Lucas says Griswold's "point is well taken" but that "a rifle is needed in open country." Lucas also reminds Griswold that farm children have chores to perform before school and that teaching them might require a little flexibility.

Clearly, the two men have little chance of hitting it off. Tensions escalate. Mark accepts punishment for another boy's hijinks and is beaten by Griswold. Finally, Mark and his pal Billy play hooky from school, eventually getting themselves stuck in an abandoned mine shaft. Billy frees himself and goes looking for Lucas; a disturbed and angry Lucas dragoons Griswold into helping him retrieve Mark. Lucas berates the effete, snide teacher: "You taught my boy rebellion!" The two men find Mark partially pinned by a downed beam in the mine. Lucas fashions a fulcrum out of a piece of wood and a flat rock while Griswold smiles and tries to comfort Mark with quotations from Archimedes. The point is clear: while Griswold talks about the virtues of science, Lucas simply *knows* them. At episode's end everyone is reconciled, with Mark offering the less-rigid, chastened Griswold a piece of candy.

Throughout the story Lucas tries to mollify Mark's new hatred of school, assuring him of the importance of education: "Everything you learn can come in handy some day." He tells Mark an apocryphal tale about how his knowledge of the story of the three hundred Spartans at Thermopylae saved his life during the Civil War. Yet Lucas, in a very American turn of mind, extols education only insofar as it serves an instrumental purpose. When one of Mark's playmates squashes berries in the nasty Griswold's textbook, Lucas cares little for Griswold's argument that "every book has a soul." Rather, he yells at Mark for forgetting that "books are expensive and difficult to freight" and tells him to get back to the schoolroom.

Throughout the teacher-parent travails, Lucas is a calm-but-firm frontier Dr. Spock. Preeminent in this quintessentially domestic drama are the contrasting masculine styles. Lucas is, as always, the handsome, proud, confident rancher in work shirt and denims, his rifle at the ready. Griswold is close to a gay stereotype, minus a lisp or high-pitched tone. He is excessively well dressed, punctilious to a fault, with no conventional signifiers of the sexually charismatic male. He is also an easterner out of touch and uninterested in the needs of farm people, an arrogant snob with no concern for the hardscrabble populace, a frontier Ichabod Crane. The Lucas-Griswold construct is hardly new to the western, but its relevance to late 1950s culture is recognizable. The centrism of the period valorizes many notions of the Jacksonian era, suggesting how the "modern style" of the 1950s isn't far removed from the early frontier era: too much "book learnin'" is seen as dangerous—to notions of rigidly defined gender and to economic enterprise. In "The Schoolmaster" the series seems to be responding to Schlesinger's concerns that excessive personal freedom is as dangerous as excessive restraint (interestingly, one could read Griswold as a nasty version of the archetypal eastern elitist whose ideas shaped postwar government and society).

The quintessential episode rendering Lucas as bedrock in the construction of frontier civilization is the two-part "The Wyoming Story" (directed by the film veteran Joseph H. Lewis), the show's most poignant demonstration of the father-son bond as essential to frontier expansion. In so doing, it associates the preservation of the domestic household with the male's effectuation of civilization. The episode is also an archetypal western narrative in its story of rescue and recovery.

At the opening of the first installment of the story, North Fork has fallen on hard times, the local cattle stricken with deadly hoof-and-mouth disease. Mark watches helplessly as two young calves die in his father's barn. The town rapidly becomes boarded up as the citizens depart. One day Micah informs Lucas of a job opening in Wyoming for an undercover agent for the federal government. According to Micah, Indians have fled the reservation and are "terrorizing settlers" with guns bought with gold stolen by a corrupt agent of the Department of the Interior. Leaving Mark behind, Lucas takes the assignment and travels to Wyoming, where he poses as an outlaw and meets the corrupt agents (Kent Taylor and Russell Thorson). A young saloon prostitute-with-a-heart-of-gold, Aggie (Enid Jaynes), learns Lucas's true identity, and the corrupt government agents find out that she knows. Like many female characters in the series, the sympathetic Aggie seems to connect to the lost love of Lucas's past live, although Aggie is too tainted for there to be more than a cordial relationship. The hoodlums beat Aggie to death in their effort to learn Lucas's true identity from her; she dies just before Lucas guns down the two villains and returns the stolen loot to the authorities.

Meanwhile, Mark is despondent, because the ranch has fallen into disrepair and he believes that his father, gone for two months, will never return. Micah gives the boy a tough-minded lecture in perseverance and faith in his father. In a moment of despair Mark senses a change in the wind, says, "Pa!" and suddenly spots Lucas on the horizon, newly bought cattle trailing behind him (he will restore the land along with his son's love). At the end of the second installment of the episode, in one of the show's most emotional moments, father and son run toward each other in extreme long shot, the camera then cutting to close-up as Mark jumps into his father's arms. In the next scene Lucas pays off old debts in town as North Fork comes back to life. Millie, the shopkeeper who acted as Mark's mother while Lucas was on his mission, invites Lucas, Mark, and Micah to dinner.

"The Wyoming Story" recapitulates the idea of the frontiersman as errant adventurer; while Lucas is far more responsible than Yancey Cravat of *Cimarron*, the two figures have much in common. The male's license to roam where he will, having whatever adventures he needs to restore not only the community but his own sense of self, are at the heart of "The Wyoming Story." Millie the shopkeeper and Aggie, the benign "dance hall girl," fulfill the familiar virgin-whore model of the female that is basic to the genre, each figure enabling the male's adventure and eventual restoration of the land. The episode is something of a throwback, refusing to problematize the knight-errant frontiersman as Ford did in *The Searchers*, also a 1950s western. "The Wyoming Story" is a tale of a father's departure and return, an affirmation of the father's basic goodness under remarkably trying conditions, and an essential consolation to both the adult and juvenile audiences at a time when the postwar nuclear family was under stress. "The Wyoming Story" is also one of the finest achievements of *The Rifleman*, capsulizing the essential concerns of the series and thereby transposing an essential theme of the western to the domestic audience of late 1950s–early 1960s television. "The Wyoming Story" appeared midway in the show's rather remarkable third season, which opened with the jarring, extraordinary "Trail of Hate," which I will discuss shortly, a far different rendering of Lucas McCain than anything developed earlier in the series.

The problematizing of the premises of the frontier experience occurs in episodes such as "Day of the Hunter," wherein Lucas and Mark encounter an aged backwoodsman, Cass Callicott (John Anderson), roughly a cross between Jim Bridger and Kit Carson. At first Lucas is delighted to meet the old man, with Lucas regaling Mark with tales he learned as a boy about the old pioneer's role in opening up the West. In short order, however, Lucas tires of the old man. At dinner Lucas becomes irate when Callicott challenges him to a marksmanship contest. Lucas refuses, prompting Callicott to propose a test of game hunting, which Lucas sees as gratuitous and wasteful, stating, "There just isn't that much game around here any more. . . . People have agreed to take only what they need." Callicott scoffs at the idea, claiming, "In my day people took what they wanted!" Lucas becomes enraged: "I know! You slaughtered all the buffalo for the hides and tongues, letting the Indians starve to death."

Eager to prove himself the better rifleman (and still of value to the new frontier), Callicott kidnaps Mark, drawing Lucas into the mountains where Callicott plans to force him into a duel to the death. Before this happens, Mark escapes and Callicott is killed by a bear. Although part of the episode is a Peckinpah-style eulogy for days gone by, the Callicott character is too eccentric and degraded to draw much sympathy. Lucas's angry remarks about the fate of the buffalo at the hands of the early mountain men turn Cooper's *Leatherstocking Tales* on their ear. Before the kidnapping Callicott regales Lucas and Mark at the dinner table with stories of his early life. Lucas sarcastically interrupts: "Didn't Daniel Boone do that?"

The episode is something of an exercise in deconstruction, calling into question the history of narration versus the official narratives of U.S. history. Lucas, who at first was charmed by the old man, acknowledging to Mark that he too enjoyed the stories of Callicott's adventures, admits to himself that Callicott embodies dangerous and false history. After Lucas's angry verbal blast about the slaughtered buffalo, Callicott, sensing Lucas to be a soft-headed liberal, responds: "One of *them*, are you??!!" As clearly as any episode, the story positions itself in the context of postwar liberalism, as much for its questioning of the American past as for its rather parenthetical statements about Native Americans and their systematic starvation by white adventurers.

Terrible Clans

The town of North Fork and the world of Lucas McCain and his son are rather consistently beset by a form of evil greater than run-of-the-mill bank robbers and brigands. Many of North Fork's enemies are degenerate psychopaths, often traveling in real or loosely formed families that can be termed "terrible clans," a notion that goes far back in western lore. The Clantons of the Wyatt Earp saga are representative examples, a savage, uneducated swarm of vermin in stark contrast to the frock-coated, stoic Earp brothers, the embodiment of postbellum Republican values. An inaugural episode of *The Rifleman*, the Peckinpah-directed "The Marshal," is representative, with its maniacal brothers (played by Warren Oates and Robert Wilke—long-term members of the "psycho" western stable) attacking Micah Torrance. The beating of Micah is accompanied by the destruction of a good chunk of North Fork, emphasizing a barbarism that the brothers turn on each other—at one point the Warren Oates character pulls a knife on his brother and drunkenly yells, "I'm gonna earmark that filthy devil!"

The town of North Fork is not far removed from Mayberry of *The Andy Griffith Show* (CBS, 1960–68); like Mayberry, North Fork was located on a Hollywood back lot street of fake veneers. Bearing no relationship whatsoever to New Mexico of the 1880s, North Fork is wholly an ideological construct. Although the town's name is taken from Sam Peckinpah's boyhood, it can be read metaphorically as explicitly not *South* Fork, a place in the netherworld, a wrong turn in the road blessedly not taken by Lucas and the town's other good people. The evil families that bedevil North Fork do so not only by committing specific crimes but also by serving as a degraded example of "white trash" that upsets the middle-class, centrist equilibrium of North Fork and the example of family set by Lucas and Mark.

Yet, just as Lucas has his dark side (see the discussion of "doubles" later in this chapter), the town and its people have their obverse in being threatened by the Other. It is instructive too that the barbaric clans, like many villains of the series, are often constructed as psychopathic. The approach to psychopathology here is retrograde, far more moralistic than clinical, suggesting a form of evil beyond reason, correctable only by force of arms. While this perspective may suggest the deep conservatism of the series, it nevertheless recognizes psychoanalysis in the manner of *White Heat* (1949); the experience of two world wars and Hiroshima had revealed to the public a sense of human nature not addressed by easy bromides.

The best episode with an evil clan is "Bloodlines." In this episode the seedy, moronic Malakie clan descends on North Fork, the three brothers (Warren Oates, Christopher Dark, John Durren) trashing the saloon and causing general mayhem until one brother accidentally shoots another. Micah, with Lucas assisting as usual, arrests the remaining brothers, who warn of their father's rage. Old Man Malakie (a wonderful turn by the comedian Buddy Hackett) arrives in town feigning regret at the destruction caused by his sons. Although Micah takes the senior Malakie seriously, he refuses to shake hands with him. Never quite the embodiment of good judgment, despite all the emphasis on wisdom honed by age, Micah turns his back on Malakie when the old man bails his sons out of jail. The sons promptly beat Micah to a pulp while the old man giggles on the sidelines ("Wouldn't shake hands with me, huh!!"). The Malakies hunt down Lucas, whom they blame for the death of the youngest son. They mistakenly shoot the dim-witted town drunk (Denver Pyle), who was temporarily employed by Lucas. A furious Micah vows justice for the "swamp rats" who buffaloed him. Lucas and Micah track the Malakies to an abandoned salt mine, where Micah packs rock salt into his shotgun shells, literally pouring salt into the Malakies' wounds before taking them into custody.

Perhaps the most instructive moment of the episode is Micah's refusal to shake hands with Old Man Malakie, whom Micah immediately sees as "trash." The father and his sons are symbols of the id, laughing at their brutality, destroying with abandon, and, above all, *looking* other than middle class. The Malakies, according to the father, were "just passing through," a statement that tends to position them as a caricature of ordinary pioneer stock, as Malakie attempts to gain Micah's sympathy by emphasizing that he is a poor widower (one of many associations with Lucas). Old Man Malakie in fact has absolute control over his sons in the manner of any frontier patriarch, their respect for him more or less total. The

Malakies are one of many mirrors reflecting the dark side of North Fork. The mirroring becomes more self-conscious as the series progresses, to a point that the show's self-deconstruction seems part of its essential trajectory.

In "High Country" Lucas and Mark run afoul of a family of hillbillies when the McCains try to right a wrong perpetrated by one of the clan's more deranged sons, Ambrose (James Coburn). Lucas assures Mark that, while "these people don't follow our ways," they are probably trustworthy because "they live close to the Good Book." The clan matriarch, Miss Morgan (Ellen Corby, later Grandma on *The Waltons* [CBS, 1972–81]), and her husband hold a ritualized makeshift trial that judges Lucas, rather than the sadistic son, guilty of transgressions. Lucas is made a slave at the hillbilly encampment and finally allowed to prove himself through a bizarre fight with torches. In short order Lucas shows the evil son to be a liar, winning respect for himself, Mark, and other "town folk." Lucas and Mark leave the hill people, promising cordial relations in the future. As is often the case in *The Rifleman*, the central point seems to be the opposite of what is stated (there is good and bad on both sides); the evil Other is at least odd, if not evil.

The most obvious lesson is that the hillbilly clan is barbaric, its laws crude and uncivilized. Before he takes on Ambrose in the torch fight, an angry Lucas declares: "You people are hypocrites." To his mind, their enslaving him has no relevance to justice and no connection to the values of civilization. Lucas refuses the clan's argument that its severe laws (and unjust punishments) are no different from the mainstream. The Bible, which Lucas marks as a signifier of the clan's probable goodness, has little relevance to a society with a "backward" (nonmiddle-class) way of life. At best, the Other might profit from lessons given by the civilization represented by Lucas, one that the Other never becomes part of.

At some points the evil clan can have upper-class, Old World affectations, as in "New Orleans Menace." Tiffauge (Akim Tamiroff) is a decadent former New Orleans vice lord, a monstrous "city slicker" who arrives in North Fork looking like a king with a large army of toadies. Tiffauge is planning to hide out at Lucas's ranch and buy it and much of the town in the bargain. Things seem hopeless until Lucas convinces one of Tiffauge's lackeys (Michael Pate) that his boss is a tyrant, whereupon the toady shoots Tiffauge, declaring Lucas *muy macho* and the dead boss "a pig."

Tiffauge's accoutrements, including champagne bottles, garish silverware, and Tamiroff's growling accent, mark him as Other as easily as the rustic barbarism marks the Malakies and various hill folk who impinge on North Fork. The heavy taint of big city vice that surrounds Tiffauge, who owned "ten blocks of the New Orleans waterfront," mark him for particularly humiliating punishment.

"New Orleans Menace" is instructive in both the formal and thematic aspects of *The Rifleman*. The episode opens with the decadent Tiffauge entourage invading the rolling, peaceful hills of Lucas's ranch. Much of the episode takes place on North Fork's cramped main street, which Tiffauge clutters with his excessive banquet table. The hyperbolic depravity that the episode ascribes to Tiffauge underscores the difference between the dangerous urban world of New Orleans and the relative tranquility of the country, over which Lucas presides. The city-country dichotomy, basic to fiction, is cleverly used throughout *The Rifleman*.

The two-part episode "Waste" (written by Robert Culp, the actor who was a close friend of Peckinpah's) combines the evil clan theme with fears of a racial Other. Lucas, Mark, and Micah become lost in a desert wasteland while returning home to North Fork. Micah is waylaid on the trail. Lucas and Mark look for him, suddenly finding themselves in a foreboding ghost town, another anti–North Fork. Mark asks his father: "Is this New Mexico or Old Mexico, Pa?" to which Lucas grimly replies, "Old Mexico, son." The town, or what's left of it, is controlled by dirt-poor banditos, grotesques whose lineage traces to *Treasure of the Sierra Madre* (1948). They immediately relieve Lucas of his rifle, taking father and son to a remote spot in the desert where they find a badly beaten Micah buried up to his neck in the sand. Lucas is forced to dig similar living graves for himself and Mark, but in a moment of pure rage that is a hallmark of his character, Lucas overwhelms his guard and makes his way back to town with his son and Micah in tow. Lucas barricades himself and Micah in a ramshackle saloon where Lucas wins a final battle against the cutthroats, first killing the none-too-bright leader, then his minions. "Waste" is complicated by a subplot involving the lead bandito's wife (Enid Jaynes), a widow who is in labor through much of the story. Lucas helps her to give birth and in the epilogue puts her on a wagon with her baby. But instead of thanking Lucas for his gallantry, she slaps him violently in the face.

"Waste" has various resonances. At one level the "waste" of the title derives from a remark by the wounded Micah, when things seem grim as he reminisces in the saloon: "This day has been a waste." However, Micah's remark has meaning only when we see it in the context of the terrible, pointless struggle between Lucas and the bandits, and the subplot of the pregnant woman's plight. At moments the episode, often shot in sweaty extreme high-contrast close-up, recalling Eisenstein or Dreyer, seems a kind of absurdist set piece out of Beckett. The slap that Lucas receives suggests the barbaric bandits' disdain for Yankee culture. Yet whatever sympathy the episode offers for the people of Mexico (which can be read as an argument against imperialism and its effects) is diluted by the controlling sense of the ghost town and its inhabitants as barbaric—if at turns woebegone—threats to normality. The episode is distinct not only for the heroes' confrontation with the evil Other but also for their immersion in a hostile environment that is the polar opposite of North Fork, which, for all its problems, remains a symbol of civilized values.

As produced, "Waste" did not represent the script written by Culp, who more fully presented the perception of Lucas, Mark, and Micah as invaders and poachers on a devastated land. In Culp's script the marshal (another marshal, not Micah) dies in Mark's arms, and the young mother spits in Lucas's face rather than merely slapping him. Having the hero spat upon was deemed much too outrageous by the show's producers. In its original conception "Waste" appears to have been among the more seriously revisionist of all TV western episodes and would thus have been intolerable to commercial television of the day. Culp has remarked that, as finally presented, "Waste" is a distortion—down to its photography—of what he wanted to say about *The Rifleman*.[5]

Terrible Fathers

The notion of terrible clans as a mirror of evil potentialities within a burgeoning civilization is tightly focused in episodes that comment on failed parenthood. With Lucas McCain always the embodiment of temperate, idealized fatherhood, *The Rifleman* offers narratives that position Lucas in contrast to deranged or otherwise failed fathers, furthering the show's moral lessons. At the same time, as I will explore, the implicit suggestion in these episodes, and the controlling theme of *The Rifleman*, is the potential violence, impatience, and authoritarian aspects of Lucas and fatherhood in general.

The importance of fatherhood to all that Lucas McCain embodies as both settler and gunfighter is explicit in the pilot episode, "The Sharpshooter." Lucas not only vanquishes the criminal element of North Fork and establishes himself in the community, he also helps a young marksman, Vernon Tippett

(Dennis Hopper), with his exploitative, manipulative uncle. When crooks murder the uncle, Lucas leaves Mark in Vernon's custody until Lucas can set things right, underscoring his role as protector of the young. The uncle's murder is relevant primarily in the narrative's erasure of the evil parent figure and in setting up the show's preoccupation with contrasting parenting styles.

A similar problem is established in "Three-Legged Terror," wherein a teenage misfit, Johnny Clover, destroys the local schoolhouse. (Clover is played by Dennis Hopper—the series put to good use Hopper's brooding bad boy persona, suggesting that Lucas's frontier values, and 1950s centrism, offer antidotes to "juvenile delinquency.") Johnny is a talented artist who loves sketching the people and events of North Fork. His tyrannical uncle (John Hoyt, who figures in several of the "terrible father" episodes) thinks that education and sketching are "unfittin'" for a man; he threatens and beats his nephew. Lucas regards schooling as necessary for the advancement of civilization, as he reminds Mark in so many words countless times. Lucas sees Johnny's drawing as a fascinating curiosity rather than impractical or effete, and as a skill probably worth encouragement.

The episode's title comes from a brief moment in the show, in which Lucas throws a picnic on his ranch to pay for the damage that Johnny caused at the school; Johnny in turn agrees to make sketches at the picnic to do his part in the fund raising. The idyll is threatened when the awful uncle appears and threatens to shoot Johnny. At the moment of this confrontation, Lucas and Mark are taking part in a three-legged race with other townsfolk who are enjoying the picnic. Still partially hobbled to Mark, Lucas picks the boy up with one arm and makes his way to his horse, where he withdraws his rifle, then hits the dirt, and, in the nick of time, shoots the uncle. The moment is one of the most memorable in the series, showing Lucas literally hobbled by parenthood even as he defends his model of it against someone seen as outdated and dangerous to the interests of his (that is, the narrative's) era.

The most extreme manifestation of the terrible father occurs in "Heller." A drunken stepfather (Peter Whitmey) ruthlessly torments two teenage children as their mother watches helplessly. The daughter, Heller (Gigi Perreau), plots the murder of the stepfather with her kid brother (Don Grady). Lucas intervenes in the nick of time as the mother stands aghast (the powerlessness of the female in crucial parenting problems is emblematic of the show). Instead of taking action physically, Lucas does so verbally—and persuasively. As Heller is about to pull the trigger, the awful stepfather whimpers on the floor. Lucas convinces Heller to put the gun down, arguing that making the man face his own cowardice and despicable nature is punishment aplenty. Note that this extreme terrible father presides over a "white trash" family; the point seems to be that the most extreme, brutal parenting occurs chiefly in the lower classes, which the show constructs as a threat to civilization overall.

"The Martinet" highlights the virtues of patience and forbearance in the face of strict discipline. A hard-bitten army officer, Captain Perry (John Hoyt), is angered by his son (Don Dubbins), who refuses to help his father track down the man who killed his brother. As it develops, Lucas killed the elder son, a confidence man and all-around ne'er-do-well, in a fair fight. Nevertheless, Captain Perry, who preaches punishment as the best discipline for his sons (he lectures Lucas on the point when Mark arrives home late from school), wants to "punish" Lucas, to use Perry's recurring term. At the episode's end the younger son, who turns out to be a preacher, makes his father understand that love is more important than discipline. The episode encapsulates the show's basic message on parenting, with Perry and Lucas representing diametrically opposed parenting styles, with Lucas's far closer to the impulses toward nurturance and understanding of the postwar era.

Harsh punishment as a remedy for disobedience in child rearing was never more overdone as a theme in *The Rifleman* than in "Eight Hours to Die." In this episode the deranged, Bible-thumping Judge Burton (George Macready) tracks down the men who arrested and hanged his wayward son. As in "The Martinet," Lucas becomes the focus of the old man's wrath because Lucas helped arrest Burton's son. This time Lucas's punishment takes the form of Mark's being kidnapped, with Judge Burton threatening to hang Mark in retribution for the Burton son's death by hanging.

After tying Lucas to a wagon, Burton lures Mark from the schoolhouse by claiming that Lucas has been injured. On their way to the McCain ranch, where Burton will mete out his vengeance, he is taken with Mark's openness. As he prepares to murder Mark, the old man is thrown from his horse and suffers a seizure. Mark looks after Burton who, in his delirium, for a moment believes Mark to be his own dead son. In a typically Herculean effort Lucas frees himself from his restraints and races to rescue Mark. Lucas arrives on the scene just as Burton points his weapon toward Mark, who is bringing water from a creek. Insane with grief and fury, Lucas throttles Burton, but Mark rushes up, showing his father that Burton merely fired at a rattlesnake. Lucas, confused by the turn of events, is about to forgive the old man when Burton suddenly dies.

Judge Burton is one of many Old Testament figures in *The Rifleman*; "Eight Hours to Die" and similar episodes are saturated with biblical revenge narratives, notions prevalent in Sam Peckinpah's major westerns. During the episode we learn that Judge Burton's son rejected him, suggesting that the boy's errant ways flowed from his father's harsh treatment. Fire-and-brimstone religiosity is repudiated, as is the notion of total obedience, unmasked in this and other episodes as ways for an inadequate parent to conceal his shortcomings. But these strict parents are never exposed as explicitly deranged, which they manifestly appear to be.

"Eight Hours to Die" takes seriously Burton's zealous, though rejected, commitment to fatherhood but exposes his failures, caused in part by too much emotionalism. While Lucas seems by far the more level-headed and caring parent, never hesitant to hug his son, his emotions are not apparent, which is not the case with the domineering parents of "The Martinet" and "Eight Hours to Die." While the fathers in these episodes appear to have replaced love with "the book" (of a military or religious sort, respectively), they are driven by overwrought feelings, for the most part stemming from narcissistic absorption with their personal failures.

Yet these terrible father episodes in some ways mirror the experiences of Lucas and Mark. At the opening of "Eight Hours to Die," Mark playfully lectures his father on the best way to prepare a coal fire. Lucas becomes testy, finally saying: "Get to school, boy," in a style and tone not dissimilar to Captain Perry's or Judge Burton's. In "Trail of Hate" Lucas embarks on a campaign of fierce, sadistic vigilantism against a team of rather dim-witted bank robbers who inadvertently hurt Mark; Lucas gains control of his temper at the penultimate moment, but the association with the terrible fathers is clear.

While *The Rifleman* is about nothing if not understanding, thoughtful parenting, it is ambivalent, and one cannot help but notice a layer of anxiety as a result. At several points in the series Lucas makes such remarks as "That boy . . . he's my strength and my weakness!" Johnny Crawford's Mark occasionally can be cloying, which puts the emphasis less on weakness than burden, because his pranks seem to bring out the ferocity of Chuck Connors's Lucas. The excuse for the unleashing of Lucas's furies is often the need to rescue or avenge Mark. The affection for Mark and the protection of home and civilization are closely linked to the special explosion of violence represented by Lucas's .44-40 Winchester, which keeps the show's tense settler-gunfighter elements in the foreground.

The mirroring function of the terrible father episodes is most explicit in "The Angry Man" and "The Long Goodbye." In the former, a rancher, Abel MacDonald (George Matthews), settles with his young son, Cary, on the edge of the McCain spread. MacDonald, like Lucas, is a widower. Cary and Mark become friends, but MacDonald wants no contact with the world and spurns Lucas's offer of friendship. MacDonald is embittered by the loss of his wife, distrustful of doctors and all symbols of civilization, which he sees as deceitful and corrupt. Although Lucas shares his own losses, and advises MacDonald about the need to persevere and be open to other people, not only to survive but to retain human qualities, MacDonald wants none of it. He is hoist by his own petard when he encircles his ranch with barbed wire and Cary accidentally becomes entangled in it. Although MacDonald refuses his son medical attention, because he blames doctors for his wife's death, Lucas and Mark take Cary to the doctor after Lucas knocks MacDonald unconscious. Cary recovers, and after a stern but compassionate lecture by Lucas, MacDonald recognizes his kinship with Lucas, opening his heart to the world as he comes to terms with his past losses.

"The Angry Man" differs from other terrible father narratives chiefly in locating the bad father's errors in simple grief rather than perverted obsessions that represent the father's character deficiencies. In "The Angry Man" the viewer is allowed another glimpse of Lucas's own losses, which the series itself won't truly explore in order to preserve Lucas's predominant stoicism and the usual machismo. More important, "The Angry Man" represents a potentiality within Lucas, although one considerably less sinister than that of "The Martinet" or "Eight Hours to Die."

"The Long Goodbye" is less about a terrible father than a misperceived one, and it engages the question of "alternate" families on the frontier. Grandpa Fogarty (Edgar Buchanan) raises his grandson, Woody (Teddy Rooney), in the wilderness, the loving pair living like hermits and in rather extreme but not quite dire poverty. The boy studies his lessons in a tumble-down shack that he and his grandfather share with a pet pig. Fogarty and Woody are friends of Lucas's and Mark's. After Mark and Lucas visit Fogarty to buy a lariat, Mark remarks to his father that the old man and his grandson have moved from place to place over the years, to which Lucas responds: "We've gotten on well by minding our own business, son."

Minding one's business becomes a theme of the episode. The women of North Fork, typical "do-gooders," regard Grandpa Fogarty as an insult to civilized values and urge Lucas and Micah to try to place Woody in a foster home. Micah is taken aback, arguing that Grandpa Fogarty "comes from a time when each man was a law unto himself," a notion that Micah and Lucas don't exactly disrespect. Lucas and Micah reluctantly visit Fogarty, who angrily rebuffs them.

Shortly thereafter Fogarty is accosted by the crazed Debo (Bill Zuckert), a tramp and small-time thief who believes that Fogarty possesses money stolen from a train when the two men were rail-riding vagrants. Fogarty protests that he never had the money. The point of this element of the story is to unmask Grandpa Fogarty's past, which did not consist of the derring-do with which he has regaled his grandson. Debo threatens Fogarty and his grandson; Lucas and his Winchester intervene in the nick of time. In the end Fogarty continues happily with his grandson.

"The Long Goodbye" picks up the "blessings of civilization" idea of *Stagecoach* and other westerns, with the episode repudiating feminine notions of child rearing—especially as these notions come between man and boy. Grandpa is plagued by "nosy neighbors" who regard him as a criminal rather than a merely impoverished man. Like MacDonald in "The Angry Man," Fogarty rejects civilization but less out of anger than a disgust with what civilization does to a sense of self. In this, Lucas has no quarrel, even as the narrative draws a clear demarcation between the prosperity of Lucas and Mark and the poverty brought on by eccentricity. "The Long Goodbye" is one of those episodes that captures the conflicting yet compatible liberal-rightist polemic at the heart of 1950s culture: the absolute individualism that was at the heart of the conquest of the West, along with some degree of conformism to middle-class mores and the acknowledgment that one of these mores, the domesticity of the female, is to be approached with great caution.

The Double

Closely associated with *The Rifleman*'s terrible fathers is Lucas McCain's "evil double," a figure represented only once in a fairly traditional doppelganger but far more frequently in shady characters with a close personal—even family—relationship to Lucas. Episodes with this theme are deeply involved with the political unconscious of the series, its semi-awareness of its hero's contradictions.

While the "double" episodes, like all others, provide comforting closure as Lucas vanquishes the enemy, they show Lucas's dark potential. At one level the episodes threaten us with a vision of how the dark potential of the United States would be realized if men like Lucas lost their senses, but what is more important is that they threaten us with a more primal vision, one that is basic to childhood anxieties, of what a parent might suddenly become. As I have mentioned, some key anxieties of *The Rifleman* come from Mark's being threatened with harm or left alone (as in "The Wyoming Story"). We are reassured by the notion that father is ultimately present, a stalwart, dependable force.

The dark fascination of the evil double episodes flows from the idea that the father may not be trustworthy, that there is at least the vague possibility that he is a monster. These episodes, as I will explain later, connect both the series and certain developments of the western during the late 1950s and thereafter to the modern horror film. The evil double episodes could not exist, of course, without a long tradition in gothic literature, modernism, and the German expressionist cinema, and the series at times borrows from all these.

Some evil doubles are relatively benevolent. In episodes like "Lariat," "The Brother-in-Law," and "One Went to Denver," we meet rapscallions who were friends of Lucas's during his younger days but who for one reason or another failed to find their way to civilization as Lucas did. "The Brother-in-Law" deals with Johnny (Jerome Courtland), the brother of Lucas's sainted late wife, Margaret. Johnny is Mark's favorite relative, his handsome Uncle Johnny, who closely resembles the boy's dead mother. Johnny is a rodeo rider whose injured back has forced him into a life of crime. Lucas learns of his brother-in-law's shenanigans and gives him a dressing-down; by the end of the episode we are assured that Johnny, who has a jovial but doomed aura around him, is not really a criminal—the episode's moral lesson is that the best people can lose their way. This cuts close to home, given how important Johnny is in the affections of Lucas and Mark.

In "One Went to Denver" Lucas and Mark are visited by an old friend, Tommy Birch (Richard Anderson), a notorious outlaw famed as the leader of the Birch Gang. Mark immediately dislikes him, but Lucas is pleased with the visit, explaining to Mark that he and Tommy "did some wild things" (which, based on the tales with which they regale Mark, primarily included murdering Indians, an idea that the episode, like the series and the TV western overall, more or less casually accepts, despite a number of liberal genuflections) and that "friendship is a strange thing." Given Lucas's moral rectitude, it seems strange indeed.

Tommy and his gang plan to rob the North Fork bank, but he has not come to visit the McCain ranch merely to gull Lucas and Mark. Tommy has a genuine affection for Lucas, evidenced in his remark that Lucas is "the only friend I've ever had." Tommy doesn't lie to Lucas about his ongoing career in crime, although he lies about the specific plans for North Fork. Mark does not witness these lies and does not need to, because Tommy is simply an object of Mark's moral loathing. He watches Tommy playfully cheat Lucas at arm wrestling; while Lucas laughs, we see the scene through Mark's youthful eyes. Lucas has a sleepless, troubled night as Tommy sleeps in the next room. The following morning Mark informs his father that Tommy has ridden to North Fork, not to Denver as he told Lucas he would the previous evening. Lucas realizes that the Birch gang plans to rob the North Fork bank. He races to town and apprehends his old friend, throwing his rifle at him to knock Tommy from his horse rather than shoot him, because of their past relationship. The scene ends with a close shot of Lucas's tormented expression.

The ostensible moral lesson of the episode is the outlaw's isolation, his inability to retain a friendship or win a child's affection because of his criminal bent. At another, almost as transparent, level is Lucas's faulty judgment of character. A more subtle issue is represented in Lucas's tossing and turning the night that Tommy stays at the ranch, as well as the arm wrestling that speaks, even (especially) in a narrative practice that represses all sexuality, to the homosocial world of the friends in "the old days." Tommy represents a world that Lucas left behind, the world that rejects civilization and upholds a form of freedom that still fascinates Lucas enough that he unreservedly welcomes an outlaw friend into his home.

"One Went to Denver" may also be seen as a comment on essential western lore. The episode's title is derived from the traditional western ballad "I Ride an Old Paint," a song featured in numerous films, including *Shane*. The singer ruminates on the fate of his two children, singing, "One went to Denver, the other went wrong." The song is plaintive, at once a song of celebration and defeat ("I'm leavin' Cheyenne"). As such, the song is perfect as an inspiration for this episode of *The Rifleman*, with its own ambivalence and unanswered questions about the life of Lucas McCain and the normality that he projects.

"Trail of Hate," which I mentioned earlier, does not contain a character who is Lucas's mischievous or corrupt opposite. Rather, it exposes the violence in Lucas's own character, a sadism turned loose out of a need to avenge his son that is classical tragedy and reveals the pathology of parenting, the drive for revenge that always has at its root the difficulties of blood ties. "Trail of Hate" is the clearest "revenge western" of the series, with Lucas tracking down a trio of inept bad guys led by Ben Stark (Harold J. Stone). Stark and his kid brother, Noley (Harvey Johnson), take Mark prisoner, forcing Lucas to help Stark and the sinister Cougar (Marc Lawrence) rob the town bank. Stark tells Noley to stay at the McCain ranch and guard Mark until the robbery is accomplished.

As it turns out, Noley is a wretched, pathetic character, abandoned by his wife and looked after by Stark, whose stealing derives mainly from his own various failures and the need to provide for his helpless brother. This notion disgusts Cougar, a deranged criminal brought along reluctantly by the Stark brothers. Noley assures Mark that he won't harm him and even helps the boy with his chores. Mark nevertheless panics and runs, in the process falling and knocking himself unconscious.

Noley and Stark panic too, when they rendezvous after the robbery, realizing, quite correctly, that they will suffer

Lucas's wrath. Lucas returns to find his injured son and brings in the doctor, who reassures him that Mark will recover. Lucas then arms himself for his rampage against the trio, saying, "I won't kill them . . . but by the time I'm through, they'll wish they were dead."

In a sequence reminiscent of Stroheim's *Greed* (1925), Lucas tracks the trio through a desert wasteland, chasing off their horses, shooting up their water canteens, and driving them to the edge of insanity as he watches their misery from distant perches, using his extraordinary rifle to full advantage. Lucas becomes an omniscient, terrible force, everywhere at once, outwitting the outlaws at each turn. The evil Cougar tries to kill Stark and is killed in the process, but one of his bullets seriously wounds Noley—as Lucas watches all this with grim impassivity. What Lucas does not know, although viewers do, is the fear and grief that Ben Stark and Noley share. We already know that Lucas's terrible hate is not really justified, since Mark's injury was an accident and Noley is a perfectly harmless person. More important, perhaps, is the reason that Stark and Noley have pursued a life of crime: Stark needs to provide for his wretchedly sad brother, and Stark is himself a failure at all other enterprises. Their employment of the psychopathic Cougar was clearly the mistake of two people who know little about the world of crime. As Noley is dying of his wounds and dehydration, Stark shouts to Lucas: "He's my brother!! He's dyin' like an animal!" Suddenly, Lucas's rage fades, and he rides up to assist the two stricken men.

In the episode's final scene Lucas helps Mark with his homework. It is obvious that Lucas is distracted. He states grimly that he could have joined Micah's posse and arrested the three men instead of turning to vigilantism and tormenting them, causing one man to die and another nearly to die. Mark seeks to console his conscience-stricken father, reminding him of his own lesson about acknowledging one's mistakes, then moving on. Lucas, still disturbed and apparently aware of the shallowness of his own admonitions for all his son's loving consolation, says, "Mark, I'll try." "Trail of Hate" is by no means *The Rifleman*'s sole representation of the frontiersman's monstrousness, but it ranks as a television rendition of some key ideas of *The Searchers*, minus the issue of race. If the idea of Lucas as deranged outlaw is implicit in "One Went to Denver," it is explicit in "Trail of Hate."

By far the clearest rendering of the monstrous double appears in "The Deadly Image," a story important not only to the history of the program but to developments in the western as it entered its revisionist phase and became associated with various conventions of the horror film. In "The Deadly Image" North Fork is visited by Earl Bantry, a psychopathic hoodlum who is clearly the worst in *The Rifleman*'s considerable rogues' gallery. Bantry is a dead ringer for Lucas McCain, played by Chuck Connors in the show's only use of rear-screen projection and other primitive "twinning" techniques. Bantry is distinguished from Lucas by an ugly scar, walrus mustache, dark makeup, and growling voice. He wears a blanket overcoat that presages the poncho worn by Clint Eastwood in the Sergio Leone westerns and carries a rifle dissimilar to but clearly evocative of Lucas's weapon. Bantry has a little sidekick, a pathetic, shifty, essentially harmless man called K.C. (Leonard Stone), whose relationship to Bantry is something like that of a familiar to an evil ogre. K.C. seems to want little from his monstrous friend but his companionship. K.C. appears to be a grown-up Mark—there is some physical similarity between Johnny Crawford and Leonard Stone. At the McCain ranch Bantry bullies Mark the same way that he badgers K.C. When K.C. tries to leave Bantry, Bantry wantonly kills him. The gentle spats that occasionally erupt between Lucas and Mark come home to roost in this fantastical mirroring.

When Bantry arrives (we're never told from where or why) in North Fork, he immediately begins to savage the town, killing with impunity, pawing women, and destroying the saloon with abandon—he is the id unleashed, an over-the-top performance by Chuck Connors that the actor clearly relishes. Bantry pummels Micah when the marshal tries to arrest him—all these moments seem to be about what is beneath Lucas's surface, what he might *like* to do if freed from the assumptions and strict conventions of the series. Bantry is a kind of monstrous adolescent, complaining, after he has cornered Lucas and Mark at their ranch, that "everybody was always telling me what to do!!" and giving vent to the kinds

The evil double: Chuck Connors as Bantry in "The Deadly Image"

of impulses that are the polar opposite of Lucas McCain's.

At first the townspeople fear that Lucas himself is the cause of the mayhem, after a few terrorized residents confuse the two men. Lucas dispels this fear but is apprehensive about the strange visitor, who eventually makes his way to the Mc-Cain ranch, apparently out of sheer desire to meet the man said to resemble him. Lucas is for a time easily overpowered by Bantry, whose ferocity makes him one of the very few truly competitive adversaries of the series; the ferocity seems to be rooted in the idea of Lucas's vulnerable confrontation with his own unconscious. In a night of mental and physical torture out of gothic fiction, Bantry reveals in a bizarre moment of self-analysis that he murdered his two older brothers. Lucas is appalled: "You murdered your own brothers??!!" Bantry, suddenly deteriorating, grabs his anguished face as he stares into a mirror, finally smashing it (another doubling effect) and yelling at Lucas: "No! You, *you* murdered my brothers!!"

During Bantry's breakdown and final tussle with Lucas, his long hair, and Lucas's, becomes disheveled. Chuck Connors's long, sideburn-adorned blond hair is one of his distinguishing features. Ordinarily, it is combed neatly back in a conservative permanent wave; in action scenes it becomes ragged and fly-about, like that of Barrymore's Dr. Jekyll. The effect was never more dramatic than in "The Deadly Image," when the suddenly unkempt appearance of Connors emphasizes the mania of both Lucas and Bantry. Lucas kills Bantry only, it seems, after he has already disintegrated, as if the self has reintegrated and repression has been restored. In the epilogue Mark tells his father and Micah, "I'll never forget that Earl Bantry," and refers to the story of Cain and Abel. Lucas opines that Bantry wanted him as a "whipping boy" since Bantry could not face his own crimes (which, of course, the episode shows us he committed). The mention of Cain and Abel, part of the biblical and other mythologies behind the doppelganger narrative, is an attempt to restore the lesson about the dangers that the Other poses to morality while acknowledging—within the limits of the show's political vision and the restraints of the form—that the dangers explicit in this episode reside in the potentialities of the self.

Race, Gender, Liberalism

The western's view of race and gender is at the heart of its most troubling features. This is certainly true for *The Rifleman*, which contains both the most retrograde aspects of the classic western and a little of the progress that the genre would make in its revisionist mode in the hands of its best directors.

As with its other themes, *The Rifleman*'s portrayal of race and gender is often rendered with a liberal, enlightened patina basic to certain postwar corporate discourses that makes all the more transparent the ignorance and hypocrisy not so much of the show but of the social consensus driving genre conventions at *The Rifleman*'s historical moment. *The Rifleman*'s accomplishment in this regard is the ability of the show's intelligence to transcend some of the narrow discourse of its era.

The genocide of the Native American population is, of course, the key issue that the western either celebrates in its classical mode or treats with some degree of evasion or disingenuousness (Ford's late films, and certain revisionist westerns on the order of *Little Big Man* [1970]). *The Rifleman* is instructive in its attempt to travel an enlightened course so representative of postwar liberalism, a guilty conscience that admits little guilt.

The Rifleman brings a major Native American character to the TV western. Marshal Sam Buckhart (Michael Ansara) is introduced in the episode titled (with a typically Hollywood sensitivity) "The Indian." Buckhart would become the lead character in the short-lived spin-off series *Law of the Plainsman* (1959–60). Ansara had played Cochise in the 1956 series *Broken Arrow*, itself based on the 1950 film. Ansara is one of those actors whose all-purpose ethnicity served him well through a variety of character roles in the 1950s through the 1980s.

We meet Sam Buckhart in "The Indian" as Lucas and Mark ride across their ranch. Suddenly, Mark yells, "Injuns!!" We see a mounted, bare-chested Buckhart, his long hair partially covered by a bandana, escorting another Native American man obviously in his custody. Mark asks his father for an explanation; Lucas tells Mark, "Whatever that one Apache did, the other one wants to settle Indian-style." Mark is excited: "You mean scalpin'?! Gosh, can I watch?" Lucas sternly reproaches Mark: "Son, our government is tryin' to teach these people to be civilized—maybe they should include you!" Nevertheless, Lucas rides up to Buckhart and his prisoner: "Hold up, Apache! What you're planning to do is not good!" Lucas speaks slowly and loudly, punctuating his statements with his forefinger, replicating the American tourist who assumes that a loud intonation will register with a person who speaks another language. Lucas warns Buckhart: "You have a grievance with this man, you tell the white man authorities, let them punish proper, savvy?"

Buckhart, shocking Lucas with his fluent, supple English, tells him that he has arrested his prisoner for assaulting an unarmed man and plans to take him to Sante Fe. Lucas is taken aback, responding, "Your speakin' proper English doesn't give you the right to arrest somebody!" Buckhart throws Lucas his badge, introducing himself by saying: "Sam Buckhart, Native American Aboriginal of the Chiracahua Apache [probably the most "politically correct" statement of early television], and Deputy U.S. Marshal for the territory." As Buckhart rides off with his prisoner, he shouts that he learned to speak "proper English" at Harvard. Mark says: "Injun marshals! What's the world comin' to?" His father answers: "Well, Harvard or no Harvard, he better not go parading his authority in North Fork!"

The scene capsulizes well the show's view of racial issues. Lucas is surprised by some of the "modern" changes in the world but adapts to them, if a little grudgingly, even as Buckhart becomes his friend. Lucas's bewilderment suggests that while the frontiersman might be "set in his ways," he is not really bigoted. Micah Torrance seems quicker to adjust to Buckhart than Lucas and chides his friend about his narrow ideas. Micah respects Buckhart for a specific reason: Buckhart represents the white man's law.

Richard Slotkin has written about the Man Who Knows Indians, a heroic type from folklore, James Fenimore Cooper, and certain renderings of historical figures such as Custer that finds its way into such characters as Ethan Edwards in *The Searchers*.[6] The Man Who Knows Indians is a white frontiersman who knows "Indian ways" so well that he can "think like an Indian" and follow tribal customs and habits with a degree of respect but ultimately uses this knowledge to gain the upper hand, usually for the purpose of killing Indians. The exposure to Indian culture gives the Man Who Knows Indians a degree of noble savagery, a contact with the primitive world that further masculinizes him without making him sacrifice his white, civilized aspect. In short, he is a better version of an Indian, one with all the pluses but none of the minuses.

Sam Buckhart is something of the inverse; he is the Indian Who Knows Whites. Buckhart was sent to Harvard by a white cavalry officer whose life he spared, an encounter that taught Buckhart the errors of racism on all sides (this puts aside, of course, state policies against Indians that had no counterpart in tribal societies). When dealing with an angry North Fork saloon crowd that is spouting anti-Indian slurs, unaware that Buckhart is Apache (at the time his long hair is

Self and Other team up: Lucas gets help from Sam Buckhart (Michael Ansara) in "The Raid"

tucked under a Stetson), Buckhart quotes Shakespeare, amending Shylock's speech from *The Merchant of Venice* by replacing "Jew" with "Indian." The crowd consists of obvious bullies and a villain shortly to be exposed; they lead a group of dim-witted locals in a small rally that worries Lucas. We see that the *real* racism belongs to the rabble and a villainous few.

Buckhart is knowledgeable not only of classical literature but of fine points of the law; he is, in short, the repository of the best virtues of white civilization. Buckhart does not use this knowledge in order to overcome the whites but rather to make white society better, acknowledging that "white man's law" is indeed the only law, a world and customs that should be embraced, with criticism limited to an occasional knowing smile. Because of this characterization Buckhart is not much of a frontiersman. Lucas, who early in the episode is afraid that Buckhart won't be able to hold his own with the town bigots once they learn his real identity, challenges him to a quick shooting match. Buckhart can't hit his target, whereas Lucas demonstrates his usual prowess, which Buckhart terms "magic."

Buckhart is accepted by Lucas and the townspeople only when he far exceeds the expectations of white society, without any of the rough edges of men like Lucas, including competence with guns—which signifies the truly masculine (the long hair and Ansara's soft features mark Buckhart as feminine)—and the possession of real power, which Buckhart serves but has little share in. Buckhart is roughly comparable to the character played by Sidney Poitier in *Guess Who's Coming to Dinner* (1960), a black man who is more middle class, well spoken, and upwardly mobile than any white character in the story. He is, above all, a character who has eradicated race as anything other than a question of skin tone. The distinction between Buckhart and the Poitier character is the extent to which the black character is integrated into the U.S. economy. The history of racism has little relevance to characters of such narratives, for all the hand-wringing about bias. *The Rifleman's* honesty resides in its straightforward if naive presentation of attempts to redress American racism.

Lucas understands Buckhart's staunch morality and helps him unmask a villain, a local businessman and leading bigot (Herbert Rudley) who is the real criminal Buckhart is pursuing, not the Apache, as Buckhart first assumed (the first hint that he is after the wrong man comes as Buckhart visits an

Apache tribe in the course of his investigation). When the local rabble (whose prejudice is portrayed as unrepresentative of North Fork as a whole, and certainly not the stumbling, foot-in-mouth ignorance of Lucas and Mark) threatens anarchy upon learning of Buckhart's identity and intention to arrest a white man, Lucas leaps on a wagon, rifle in hand, making an angry, sarcastic speech about why the town may as well shoot Micah too since its contempt for the law is so great. Micah smiles knowingly from the sidelines, always the ineffectual bystander to Lucas's real lawman.

Lucas is only too happy to go to bat for Buckhart once Lucas perceives Buckhart's solid commitments to "the law" and the conventions of white society. That is when the world of *The Rifleman* allows Buckhart to retain his Apache garb and full identity, which, after all, offers the character as exotica, a key function of Native Americans in white narratives.

If Buckhart needs Lucas to enforce the law and do his job, Lucas has no real use for Buckhart in "The Raid," the episode that features Buckhart's return. "The Raid" is a mini version of *The Searchers*. An Apache warrior who wants a son kidnaps Mark. The people of North Fork form a search party that includes Lucas, Micah, and Sam Buckhart, who talks endlessly about Apache lore and stealth. He confirms a bigot's comment that "the Apache kill their prisoners," raising the show's tension. Lucas suffers a head injury during the search that knocks him out of the action; Buckhart assures Lucas that he can move faster alone, that he knows the Apache concept of the "quiet hunt," and that he will bring Mark back. But Lucas is having none of it. Although almost delirious from his wound, Lucas follows Buckhart at a distance, saving him with a volley from his rifle when Buckhart bumbles his way into the Apache camp. Buckhart may be capable of arresting cowardly white bigots, but only Lucas's rifle can take care of crazed savages who violate white male patriarchy and blood succession.

Mexico and Hispanic culture are specters in *The Rifleman*, represented as much by terrain as characterization. As in many classic westerns, Mexico is a desert wasteland, a place misused or left barren until the arrival of Anglo civilization—its opposite is a verdant Eden ripe for romance and adventure—a dialectic of "burnt-over desert" and a land "green and growing" offered by Davy Crockett (John Wayne) and Jim Bowie (Richard Widmark), respectively, in Wayne's *The Alamo* (1960).

Desert wasteland, stricken by poverty as well as base criminality, is the controlling image of Mexico in *Rifleman* episodes such as the two-part "Waste," which I discussed earlier. "Waste" is among the show's more complicated meditations on Mexico, its dark expressionist style reflective of the debased cruelty of the banditos, Lucas's rage against them, and the rage of Mexico against Lucas/Anglo society, as suggested in the young mother's slapping Lucas after he delivers her baby in the final scene. The episode suggests Mexico's rejection of a "helpful," philanthropic Anglo culture that soothes its conscience by individual acts of charity that in no way right economic wrongs. "Waste" might be *The Rifleman*'s most self-aware repudiation of a bogus liberalism.

Such repudiations are by no means consistent in the series. In "The Vaqueros" Lucas and Mark are stranded in a parched stretch of Mexico, waylaid by a group of we-don't-need-no-stinkin'-badges banditos led by a leering, sadistic boss (Martin Landau) whose intentions in taking Mark hostage seem pederastic. Thus the banditos are a threat to American masculinity as well as life and property. Lucas is stripped of his shirt and boots (that he is not left naked is an obvious function of the production code) and hanged by his wrists. With his usual superhuman will, Lucas frees himself, trudges across the desert to the small village that is the robbers' roost, reclaims his rifle, which was stolen by the vaqueros, and massacres the lot of them in his archetypal volley of Winchester lead. The townspeople, including an old wise man (Vladimir Sokoloff, who perfected the role in *The Magnificent Seven* [1960]), are cowed by the bandits and by Lucas, but they finally offer Lucas help and then their gratitude as liberator. "The Vaqueros" is a typical narrative of Americans as benign interventionists, their intervention justified by injustices perpetrated against them. Lucas's intervention is pure, not nearly as compromised as in *They Came to Cordura* (1959) or *The Wild Bunch* (1969).

"The Gaucho" presents what at first seems to be the show's most forthright comment on racism. An Argentine family buys a ranch close to the McCains', and the son, Manolo (Perry Lopez), befriends Mark and entertains him with powerful *bolas*, an Argentinean lariat that consists of a rope with two or more weighted balls (usually leather-covered stones) on its end. A local troublemaker (Stuart Randall) upsets the local social equilibrium by referring to Hispanics as "pepperguts," a term that Mark picks up, to his father's great anger. Lucas apologizes for Mark, which leads to the friendship between Mark and Manolo.

As it develops, Manolo is also a bigot, calling Lucas and others "gringos." He objects to his sister's dating a local rancher, who is mysteriously killed. It is at first assumed that the murderer is a local redneck, until Manolo, the young gaucho, admits his guilt with maniacal glee, attempting to kill Lucas with his *bolas*, and falling on his own knife in the scuffle that ensues. Manolo is somewhat vindicated by his father's explanation that Manolo's mother was killed by an outlaw, apparently an Anglo.

The episode attempts to draw the lesson that "there's good and bad on both sides," a banality that might be an instruction for the child audience but sorely fails to attain the wider ideological reach that *The Rifleman* often attempts, its racial politics called into question by the imposition of a lesson frequently repeated in the series.

Still, the episode has a compelling little subtheme that gives added resonance. The episode opens with Mark hectoring his father for a rifle, which Lucas refuses to buy for the boy. In the epilogue, with Mark mourning his newfound friend Manolo and confused by his violence, especially after Lucas's lessons in tolerance, Lucas attempts to console Mark by offering to buy him the rifle that he wanted (without ammunition). Mark decides against it, tearfully telling his father that if he waits until he is older, he'll appreciate it more. With the "The Gaucho" a tale of guns, *bolas*, and knives, the moment suggests that Mark has forsaken violence, at least temporarily.

In a variety of episodes, Lucas preaches tolerance, often when the threat is obscure or rather bland, as in "Duel of Honor," in which an Italian nobleman (Cesare Danova) is heckled by a local redneck (Jack Elam) for his "fancy ways." The threat that the nobleman represents to North Fork stems primarily from his intellectualism (not an inconsiderable problem in the western—the fate of Doc Holliday in *My Darling Clementine* [1946] and Hatfield in *Stagecoach* may be instructive) and effete manner, permitting a rather spontaneous if quizzical support from Lucas. The redneck is scared off when he sees the nobleman's prowess with eighteenth-century dueling pistols.

In "Two Ounces of Tin," one of two episodes featuring Sammy Davis, Jr., the consequences of racism are explored and somewhat evaded. As the episode opens, a dark-clad gunfighter, Tip Corey (Davis), rides into North Fork. A local laborer runs up to Micah Torrance yelling: "Marshal, what's *he* doin' in town?!" Because Corey is played by one of the 1950s' few African American celebrities, it is hard not to feel, then or now, that the comment refers to the character's race.

Corey, as it develops, is a notorious gunfighter. Micah confronts him; Corey pulls his gun with incredible speed, letting Micah know how seriously he is outclassed. Corey also humiliates the hapless marshal—who is always in need of assistance in any event—by demanding that Micah throw his badge into the dirt before sundown. Corey then rides off. He is befriended on the trail by Mark McCain. As a reward for Mark's help with a lame horse, Corey dazzles Mark with fancy shooting tricks. Corey tells Mark that he was once an entertainer with Buffalo Bill's Wild West Show.

Suddenly, Lucas appears, sternly ordering Corey off the property and informing Mark that Corey is a "killer." Unknown to anyone else in the narrative, Corey travels to a cemetery where he visits his father's grave, marked "unknown." He tells his dead father that he has taken revenge for some grievance, then weeps bitterly at his fate as a hated gunman and becomes more overwrought still as he vents his anguish at being alone in the world. He cries out to his dead father ("I'm lonely, Pa!"), clearly establishing a further link to Mark. It is a remarkable moment for the TV western; two versions of the Other have been displayed and overturned as the show comments on both race and the outlaw gunfighter.

Corey returns to North Fork, where Lucas is wearing Micah's badge while Micah is out of town to give a deposition in another community. Per the show's convention, Lucas is represented as the real moral force in the town, taking on the badge of authority in a serious crisis. This focuses Corey's ire on Lucas; he gives Lucas the same ultimatum that he gave Micah in the first scene. Obviously, Lucas views the diminutive gunfighter with contempt, although Lucas is concerned about Corey's skill.

Mark, who likes Corey, visits him in an effort to understand his obsession with the marshal's badge, which Mark's father is now forced to defend. Corey tells Mark that years earlier Corey's father tried to help an Indian woman who was being molested by a drunken mob. He instructed the young Tip to fetch the marshal, who refused to help. The mob killed Corey's father and the woman. Thus Corey's hatred is focused not on Micah or Lucas but on the town and its institutions. During the meeting with Mark, Corey mentions a grave near town, obviously his father's. Mark says he knows the grave and that he places flowers on it, because it is the only marker inscribed "unknown." Mark has impressed Corey yet again. Corey's affection for Mark, along with an increased sense of hopeless resignation, prompts a fatal decision. In a final street confrontation, Corey gives his ultimatum to Lucas but then draws deliberately slowly, allowing Lucas to kill him—a rare moment in the series when we see Lucas as less than competent.

The episode is far more complicated than this synopsis conveys, although the implications of Corey's conflict with North Fork and its authority should be clear enough. Mark is the only person in the town who sympathizes with Corey, and this does not change even in the epilogue. Even after Lucas knows more about Corey's past, the most he can offer is a "there but for the grace of God" homily. North Fork, in Corey's recounting of his youth and in the period of the narrative, seems wholly contemptible.

The episode constructs the gunfighter not only as social outcast but as an outcast whose destructive vision seems wholly justified. The gunfighter-as-Other is amplified by the casting of a celebrated African American actor, one who was torn by his identity and social-political convictions.[7] Corey's recounting of his father's murder—which we cannot help but envision as a lynching—is told by Corey in his father's voice, which has the deferential tone of a postbellum freed slave. Corey's life as a criminal began in vigilantism against a society that would not protect minorities—and once we learn that the murders that Corey seeks to avenge involved both his father and an Indian woman, it is impossible to pretend that

Sammy Davis was cast solely because of his star power and well-known fast-draw stunts in Las Vegas.

The association of criminality with the marginalization of racial minorities is fairly basic to fiction. The racial aspect of the episode, and its attempt to contain it and restore normality and justice, are central to the dilemma of the episode and *The Rifleman*. "Two Ounces of Tin" can be seen as the show's response to the civil rights movement, acknowledging that the real wrongs stem from the denial of an ignorant, bigoted white society. Yet the show cannot acknowledge the rebellious racial Other as anything more than a troubled troublemaker, however sadly unjust his situation. That the episode ends with extreme uneasiness, with Corey calling out "Pa!" as he dies in Lucas's arms, followed by Lucas and Mark at Corey's graveside, is a tribute to the integrity of a show whose competition dealt in dogmatic absolutes.

Race and gender converge in "The Boarding House," an episode written and directed by Sam Peckinpah in one of his few returns to the series after the initial episodes. Julia (Katy Jurado), a Mexican American woman who runs North Fork's new boardinghouse, is accosted in the street by Lucas, who recognizes her as a card cheat who ran a crooked faro game in another town. Julia is humiliated and walks away. Lucas speaks to Micah about Julia's "bad influence" on North Fork. Micah adopts his older-and-wiser posture, one of his few long suits; he refuses to pass judgment on Julia's former life.

The episode is remarkable for portraying Lucas as an arrogant prig; when he goes to Julia's house to inform her that North Fork "doesn't need her kind," Julia, now infuriated, slaps his face, forcing an apology. There is a strong suggestion that Julia should be read as a former prostitute—that her role is transformed for 1950s television in the same way that Miss Kitty becomes merely a "saloon keeper" for the many years of *Gunsmoke*. The suggestion is even stronger when Julia's former employers show up with plans to force Julia back into vice, with her ex-boss wielding a switchblade and looking as much like a pimp as television standards and practices would allow. Lucas intervenes, forces Julia's bullying ex-cronies out of town, and bolsters Julia's legitimacy with the bluenose citizens.

What is most remarkable about "The Boarding House," and almost all episodes dealing with the plight of women, is Lucas's utter disinterest in them as sexual beings. On the one hand, we might say that Lucas is among the more enlightened specimens of masculinity, able to have friendships with women without needing axiomatically to associate with them sexually. He stoically honors his late wife (or says he does), like Will Munny in *Unforgiven* and a whole line of western heroes. On the other hand, he represents a hyperbolic rendering of the homosocial world of the western, with women rather suspect except when kept in precisely defined roles. Certainly, the episodes that are the most fun (that is, dangerous, intriguing) have little to do with women. In the exemplary "The Wyoming Story" Micah tells Millie to "keep quiet" while he gives Mark a stern lesson. Although two women figure prominently in the series—Millie, the storekeeper, and Lou Mallory, the hotel owner—neither has much of a relationship with Lucas, even though both seem constructed as his "love interest."

In episodes in which women's interests are directly at issue, they are treated either with a clenched-teeth tolerance or caricatured as femmes fatales, temptresses whose aims are wholly destructive. In the latter, as in film noir, the female's attractiveness and sexualization are in direct proportion to the danger that she represents. As a symbol of phallic authority, Lucas's rifle is never more central than in such episodes. Lucas's violent interventions suggest a rejection of the female even when he works to secure justice for women.

A representative portrayal of the female occurs in "The

Woman," the very title suggesting an alien, bizarre interloper. Adele Adams (Patricia Barry) is North Fork's new schoolteacher, a suffragette who rallies the women in the town—the show addresses feminism directly here, as it would be on the rare occasions when feminism was addressed at all in 1950s television. The episode opens with Mark stricken with a bad case of the measles, his father humoring him as Adele gives him *Moby-Dick* (which may have been a sly joke, not uncommon in the show) to read, telling Mark that it is a tale about a man "consumed by hate." Mark's fever and Adele's sudden arrival with Melville's novel, a quintessential American masculinist adventure, establishes the episode's complicated issues. Immediately, female sexuality is presented both as an erotic fever blighting male judgment and a plague that disrupts community equilibrium. There is also the notion of the female purely as an erotic being, her demands, including those associated with social justice, always tied to male sexual frustrations born of patriarchy's own assumptions and laws. *Moby-Dick* has relevance not only to the villain of the episode but to elements of Lucas's personality and those of North Fork men. Adele also gives Mark and Lucas some suffragette pamphlets. Commenting on the notion of women voting, Lucas jokes that "it's a little like racing a stallion with a cow."

As Lucas visits North Fork to buy supplies for the homestead, the notion of feminism-as-plague becomes a bit more explicit. At the general store Lucas learns that Hattie, the proprietor, has ordered a shipment of "bloomers," suddenly much in demand by the town's women. Lucas looks at the garment—women's underwear with associations with both male trousers and male genitalia—with bemused dismay. While humor surrounds these moments, they and the opening scene appear as if signifiers of a slowly encroaching disease, like the harbingers of hoof-and-mouth disease and other disasters that threaten North Fork in earlier episodes. As it develops, the threat that Adele represents is embodied not just in her activism but in her sexual allure. Another "white trash" family, the Healey clan, pursues Adele, wanting to "tar and feather" her (this medieval punishment summons up images of sexual humiliation as well as witch burning) for jilting their youngest son, Garth (Paul Carr), whose immaturity caused him to misinterpret Adele's friendship. Not wishing to cause trouble or face the Healeys' wrath, Adele decides to leave town, telling Lucas and Micah that North Fork is a "narrow, wicked town filled with narrow, wicked people," a sentiment that we are convinced she actually believes.

Lucas convinces Adele to stay on as the schoolteacher just as the dangers escalate. Old Man Healey (Paul Westerfield) plans to horsewhip first Adele, then Garth for his weakness in not making Adele accept him. Garth then summons the courage to face down his father, who is suddenly murdered by the imbecilic middle son, who has tired of his father's constant harassment. The episode concludes with Hattie paying a visit to the McCain ranch, where Lucas is now down with the measles. Mark is reading to him from one of Adele's suffragette pamphlets. Lucas, mildly exasperated, says, "Can't we go back to *Moby-Dick*?" Mark is shocked when he realizes that Hattie is wearing trousers, finally agreeing with his stricken father and closing the episode on a comic note.

The episode is a thirty-minute, half-serious look at patriarchal civilization that contains the suggestion that, as a means of enforcing male authority, Lucas, for all his limitations, is preferable to the "old" patriarchy, as represented by the Healeys and their sadistic threats of violence. It is also reasonable to see the episode, particularly with a half-century of hindsight, as a condemnation of Lucas's false tolerance—he, as much as Healey, may be the cruel Ahab of the story—and of the limitations of the show's liberalism.

These limitations are made clear as the episode enunciates its view of feminism. Adele describes her past history while making an omelet for Lucas and Mark; she states that women will soon be "proud, beautiful, and free." While Hattie calls men "benevolent tyrants" after reading one of Adele's pamphlets, she speaks of a "woman's intuition" as she encourages Lucas to pursue the Healeys. Above all, Adele carries the aura of disrupter of equilibrium. While she bears no guilt, her very presence is a threat, first as an activist, then as a sexual being. It is difficult to regard her as a Madonna-protector of the hearth typical of the western and folklore.

The female as temptress is the topic of "Nora." Nora Bradford (Julie Adams) is an attractive woman from Lucas's early life who comes to North Fork feigning poverty. Her true motive for the trip is to seduce and marry (and then kill) Lucas to get money for her degenerate gambler boyfriend, who is in debt to a thug named Morgan (Murvyn Vye). Nora is a convincing con artist, languishing in her hotel bed à la Camille as she tells Lucas a tale of woe about no money for food, her loneliness after the death of a cruel husband who married her for her wealth (which, we learn, she squandered in her sybaritic lifestyle with her lover).

Mark, always on the lookout for a mother, takes to Nora's beauty and charm, while his father, always skeptical of women, remains kind but aloof as usual. Nora meanwhile pretends to be sexually interested in Morgan, convincing him to assist her in ambushing and killing Lucas. When Lucas comes upon them unexpectedly, Nora rips her dress, suggesting that Morgan tried to rape her and forcing Lucas to her defense. Then she shoots Morgan, revealing to Lucas that he was had. We later learn that Nora's boyfriend has won a huge sum of money at poker, making her entire nefarious scheme unnecessary. In the epilogue Lucas sits alone by his fireplace, telling Mark that sometimes one can be disappointed to learn of an old "friend's" true character. The final shot of Lucas's melancholy face suggests an uncommon romantic longing as much as disappointment with Nora's perfidy.

"Nora" has some instructive moments, including her statement to Morgan that "you'd be amazed how many 'ladies' dream of being saloon girls." The remark, suggesting the sexual fantasies of women, seems extraordinary, given the period in which the show was produced. Nora's realization that her suddenly rich boyfriend will now leave her provokes her sobbing statement that she will be "all alone."

While the show explicitly constructs the sexual female as a danger, associating seduction with murder in the most literal configuration of the femme fatale, Nora is still a figure of some sympathy. "Nora" is an episode in which the show's political unconscious becomes manifest, revealing the need to condemn what it cannot help but recognize. Lucas's continued aloofness and apparent immunity to sexual temptation seem to reflect this convention of the western, which certainly was within the postwar liberal consensus. The male must try for a neutral position that retains male privilege while not upsetting the demands of a new domestic culture (the 1950s) that recognizes the changing situation of women.

The Rifleman's notion of a domestic frontier is caught in a stalemate, as the show appeared at the cusp of important sociopolitical changes in the United States. The show is an acknowledgment, by way of corporate liberalism, of those changes, and the need for the western, that quintessential genre of white male privilege, to relinquish some ground. I do not mean to suggest that this relinquishing is altogether devious or intellectually dishonest. There is insufficient evidence of anything like dishonesty, and intent is often hard to measure. The level of intelligence is often compelling, and the show is crucial, with all its weaknesses, to understanding the social and other discourses of its day. With its contributions from Dick Powell, Sam Peckinpah, Arnold Laven, Joseph Lewis, and others, *The Rifleman* is an example not only of the electronic media as sociopolitical nexus but also as superb collaborative art.

The female as temptress: a young con artist (Julie Adams) seduces a quizzical Lucas in "Nora"

The Gunfighter as Fetishist

A few words are in order about *The Rifleman's* rifle, and about the notion of the West as constructed by the TV western, with its peculiar ideas of masculinity and community, which often seem at odds with the genre's conservative ideological agenda.

Lucas's rifle might be said to represent the sealed homosocial universe of the western in the weapon's eccentric design—one with a history, to be sure, since John Wayne carried a Winchester with a large loop lever action in *Stagecoach, Hondo* (1953), and again in *Rio Bravo* (1958), and Robert Mitchum carried one in *El Dorado* (1967). It is not overreading the sexual symbolism of this weapon to say that the loop action suggests the scrotum, while the long barrel of the rifle is the archetypal phallus. That Ringo, John T. Chance, and Lucas McCain should use such a weapon speaks to issues beyond the obvious ones of out-of-control testosterone, the primacy of the male, and the tendency to scream this primacy in the western, the most masculine genre.

In *Rio Bravo* Chance says he carries a rifle because he has found that "some [gunslingers] are faster with a short gun," one of the first clues that this film will be turning conventions of the western on their ear. Indeed, this film is celebrated for playing freely with the codes of the genre, offering a lawman not so fast on the draw, a world relatively static. *Rio Bravo*'s real innovations might be best understood in comparison to the TV western's, as the TV western was defining the genre when *Rio Bravo* was being made. With its confined sense of space, cheesy costumes, back lot town, and eschewing of many of the cinematic genre's conventions, *Rio Bravo* indeed *looks* like a TV western.[1] The insulated male world populated with male beefcake and pretty boys (Dean Martin and Ricky Nelson) offers potent gay material (one can hardly say subtext) as it explores male "codes of honor" (and much more is encoded) in the film's fullest association with the TV western.

Chance's omnipresent stylized rifle is a signifier that alerts the audience, especially viewers watching it more than once, to the western as a form that is perhaps less about male professionalism (the traditional element of the genre that is the ostensible subject of *Rio Bravo*) than male love, replete with serenades ("My Rifle, My Pony, and Me") and kisses (Chance's pecking Stumpy on the head). Of course, the director Howard Hawks stumbles upon this implicit content while exploring the assumptions of the male world. Indeed, the homosocial material appears to follow axiomatically from Hawks's integrity in this exploration, even if he would doubtless vehemently repudiate his ultimate findings. (*Reservoir Dogs* [1992] is a postmodern *Rio Bravo* that takes on these issues forthrightly.)

Specialized weaponry, particularly as the western reaches television, takes on a certain kinkiness, along with a form of artifice that affects the TV western in general. Weaponry associated with the skills of heroes dates to classical art; in the case of the TV western, odd weaponry creates a certain cachet for a series, separating one hero from another. Yet the weaponry, like costuming and mise-en-scène, has an eccentricity bordering on the absurd, underscoring the hermetic world of the TV western, connecting it to both the juvenilia of the kiddie shows (the Lone Ranger, Roy Rogers) and the "drugstore cowboy" sense of the West that would become standard in the iconography of gay culture. Much of *The Rifleman* has the ring of authenticity, down to the period books by Lucas's armchair. The extreme artifice of many TV westerns might be attributed to connections with the spangled look of the singing cowboys of the 1930s, with their own connections to Wild West shows, the rodeo, and vaudeville. The look was modified to achieve its "adult" aspect and to acknowledge the deep debt to film-makers such as Ford. The retention of artifice is in part concerned with the often marginal production values of the TV western; the homage to the male, and in particular the male body, seems to have another agenda.

Lucas's form-fitting jeans, and the fringed, frilled, and custom-cut costumes of his TV western counterparts, speak to a rejection of, even a disdain for, realism. Weapons, like clothes, suggest less the advantage that a certain gun gives its owner (the manifest rationale for its use) than the fetish value of the thing. Lucas's rifle, while distinctive as the Excalibur of TV western weaponry, is hardly unique in this regard. Josh Randall (Steve McQueen) of *Wanted: Dead or Alive* wore a "mare's leg," a severely cut-down rifle worn like a pistol. Johnny Yuma (Nick Adams) of *The Rebel* wore a sawed-off shotgun as a pistol. Paladin (Richard Boone) of *Have Gun, Will Travel* wore a nickel-plated, long-barreled Colt in an elegant black holster adorned with a silver chess knight. Paladin also switches from the effete clothes of his erudite, hotel-dwelling public persona into the black costume of his mercenary other self. *Have Gun, Will Travel* is remarkable in its sense of the gunfighter having a self that can be unveiled only in the relatively barren and barbaric wilderness, where the hero's profession prevents people from raising too many questions about this odd change of identities.

The list of the TV western's various forms of quirkiness is long. Suffice it to say that weapons and the rest of TV western decor represent a fetishism that constitutes a "new religion" for those who partake of the world of the fetish, as Wilhelm Stekel notes.[2] Stekel notes how fetishism is as much about a peculiar asceticism as it is "an open battle with every form of authority," a preference for a closed world rather than the social world of integrated sexual life. Such may describe the pre-

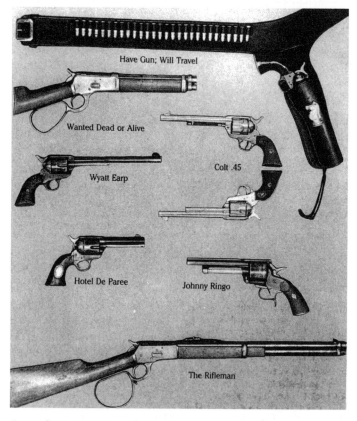

Have Gun; Will Travel

Wanted Dead or Alive

Wyatt Earp

Colt .45

Hotel De Paree

Johnny Ringo

The Rifleman

Guns as fetish objects from the TV western

pubescent male, but does this account for the acceptance by an older audience of the synthetic vision of the TV western, with its false-front towns and dandified (even in work clothes) fast-draw heroes? The "closed world" described by Stekel is instructive, if we regard the enclosed homosocial/homosexual space of the TV western as safety-valve escapism.

Little about the TV western associates it with any Brechtian alienation effect, such as one finds in Douglas Sirk's florid melodramas that emphasize the garishness of U.S. culture. In the absence of such devices, one must look elsewhere to account for the excessive artifice of the TV western (beyond low-budget production values) and their kitsch portrayals of the cowboy and the frontier. Lucas McCain and his fancy rifle represent a relatively conservative turn within a tradition that includes gunfighters with jeweled hatbands, frilled shirts, blue frock coats cut to accommodate prominent ivory-handled revolvers, buckskin suits fitted so tight that the actors wearing them today would be (and often are) subjects for nostalgic homage in gay beefcake magazines. Indeed, the homosocial aspect of the TV western, with its emphasis on the male physique, male clothing, and frontier as male playland, tends to run counter to much of the ideological agenda that the TV western borrows from cinema and the official culture of the 1950s.

While the final legacy of the TV western might well be a form of resistance to the mainstream, it serves to remind us how limited the sites of resistance in U.S. culture really are. Pointing out contradictions within mass culture, a constant in any case, reminds us of the dangers in the postmodern moment of replacing politics with cultural study, of assuming that this or that fluke within the culture industry is a harbinger of social change, at a time when the American left remains atomized, and progressives make only occasional, compromised gains.

95

On the Horror Film
and the Western:
Chuck Connors After *The Rifleman*

As suggested earlier, the gothic and morbid elements of *The Rifleman* are fairly easy to spot, as is the way the series conveys the fragility of the American community, one that would nearly disintegrate with the Vietnam incursion and the crises of the 1960s and 1970s.

Robin Wood has argued persuasively that westerns such as *Man of the West* (1957) prefigure *The Texas Chainsaw Massacre* (1974).[1] The frontiersman hero of Anthony Mann's extraordinary western (played by Gary Cooper, one of the key American icons of the old studio system) turns out to be the fiendish son of a monstrous criminal father, and the kin of an outlaw gang established as a barbaric clan.

In *Man of the West* the hero remains the hero, forced only temporarily to revisit his savage past, just as Lucas McCain remains the benign father to his cheerful, obedient son, with eruptions of discontent appearing sporadically as aberrations. In *Chainsaw Massacre*, Tobe Hooper's pivotal horror film, the frontier is wholly desiccated, berserk, and merciless, the line between self and Other vanished, yet the film is an authentic western, its subject the homestead, the family, and the horrible state of the decayed frontier community in late

97

twentieth-century America. Indeed, the western appears to be the true progenitor of the modern horror film, because many of the most distinguished examples of the latter, at least since *Psycho*, have been concerned with the fate of the American community, its heroes and villains, and the easy assumptions that once supported their characterizations.

It seems to me that by now various sources have established the connections between the western and the horror film, but I will make a few brief additional comments here by way of noting the remarkable contributions of the star of *The Rifleman*, Chuck Connors. Connors's performance on the series, and the trajectory of his career, is an emblem—perhaps an idiosyncratic one—of ideas more explicit in films such as *Man of the West*.

A former player for the Brooklyn Dodgers and Boston Celtics before beginning a film career in the early 1950s, Chuck Connors had one of the more problematical star images in postwar film history. Although he seemed tame enough in quiet character parts in films such as *Pat and Mike* (1952), his huge stature and long face made him appear to be a human monster on the order of Rondo Hatton and similar second-string actors who populated the early American horror film solely because of their strange countenances. More important, Connors projected a volatility that threatened to go out of control. One film reference source terms Chuck Connors a "tough guy American hero/villain, his thin smile being adaptable to friendship or menace."[2]

Known in some Hollywood circles (and sometimes on the set of *The Rifleman*) for his occasional cruel humor and sometimes out-of-control eccentricities, Connors was at times a figure of menace off the screen as well as on. Indeed, menace accounted for a good deal of Connors's career. In 1958, the year Connors began work on *The Rifleman*, he played a bullying ranch hand in William Wyler's *The Big Country*. Following *The Rifleman*, obviously the high point of his career, Connors starred in a few other series (*Branded, Arrest and Trial, Cowboy in Africa*) before trying for more movie roles. Connors, never a candidate for leading man status because of his physique and ambiguous smile, concentrated on character roles in film and occasionally television.

According to the director David Schmoeller, Connors intended to parlay his threatening physique and face—with its ever-lengthening lantern jaw—into recognition as the "new Boris Karloff,"[3] a status that never truly materialized. But in films such as *The Mad Bomber* (1972), *Kill Them All and Come Back Alone* (1970), *Soylent Green* (1972), the celebrated TV miniseries *Roots* (1977), and, above all, Schmoeller's small film *Tourist Trap* (1979), Connors created a small legacy as a screen monster. These roles never obliterated *The Rifleman*, which has grown in reputation with the video/DVD revolution and the nostalgia of the baby boom generation. Rather, these roles allowed Connors to amplify notions within that series and the western. In retrospect, Connors's role as Lucas in *The Rifleman* seems an oddity, given his predilection for the horrific in many of his screen roles. He was a talented, largely self-trained actor who grasped spontaneously the requirements of Lucas McCain, the gentle father and stern defender of justice. He was in his thirties at the time of *The Rifleman*, the full menace of his physique (which indeed had aspects of Frankenstein's monster, with the high, straight brow, massive jaw, and huge body) not yet marked by the deteriorations of age. His attempts to become the new Boris Karloff, although never realized, produced some revelatory work, for both Connors and American genre cinema, of which *Tourist Trap* is especially instructive.

A horror film much influenced by such 1970s films as *The Texas Chainsaw Massacre* and *The Hills Have Eyes* (1977), *Tourist Trap* uses a Hansel-and-Gretel narrative to tell a disturbing tale of the American backwater, with a group of young people stumbling onto a roadside eatery and frontier museum

The emerging monster in a changed America: Chuck Connors post-*Rifleman* in *The Mad Bomber*

owned by a man named Slausen (Connors). A hillbilly rendering of *House of Wax* (1952), Slausen's museum contains effigies of Stonewall Jackson, George Armstrong Custer, and Davy Crockett that, with other bizarre mannequins (actually the bodies of the dead reanimated by Slausen), come alive to terrorize and annihilate the young tourists.

In *Tourist Trap* and other horror films of the post-Vietnam period, the bad conscience of the frontier returns to haunt the present world. Slausen, as it turns out, is a lunatic, periodically taking on the identity of his monstrous brother—the film sketches more fully the implications of *Rifleman* episodes like "The Deadly Image."

During the film's production Schmoeller learned something of Connors's rather puerile (or worse) humor. For unknown reasons Connors asked Schmoeller whether he recalled *The Rifleman*, in particular the famous title sequence. Connors asked whether Schmoeller remembered the rifle, especially the frames in which he held the rifle near his groin in the explosive opening. Then he said to Schmoeller, "You remember how I cocked it, and cocked it, and cocked it?"[4] Schmoeller was startled by the actor's perversity. This, coupled with Connors's bullying style ("Wanna fight?") was meant to intimidate the director, made Schmoeller very cautious of the otherwise talented actor.

Percy Adlon's *Salmonberries* (1991), Connors's last film appearance, is an interesting final chapter for *The Rifleman*, the western, and this monograph. Adlon's avant-garde narrative, like his earlier *Baghdad Café*, is too complex on issues of gender, race, and the conquest of the American frontier to summarize adequately here. To be very brief, the story, set in a frozen Alaskan rural community, concerns Kotz, an androgynous Eskimo (k.d. lang) who is attempting to find her origins with the help of a matronly librarian (Rosel Zech), who is disturbed by her own past history in East Germany.

Looming over the narrative is Bingo Chuck (Chuck Connors), owner of the local bingo parlor and saloon. Bingo Chuck, as it turns out, is the father of many illegitimate children, including Kotz. Although in many respects pathetic (conveyed well by Connors's now-stooped physique and haggard expression), Bingo Chuck conveys menace in his growl of a voice; he is an emblem of the white European "settler" whose influence on the native population of Alaska, the fabled "last frontier" of the United States, has been devastating. He now presides, in wizened form, over a bingo game in a gray wasteland, the broken, sad remains of entrepreneurial capitalism. *Salmonberries*' resolution is crushing, poignant, and terrible, as Kotz confronts her father but is ultimately repelled by Bingo Chuck's dishonesty and manipulation.

On a much more romantic level, the telefilm *Lonesome Dove* (1989), perhaps the last great classical western, excuses the widowed, stoic father Woodrow Call (Tommy Lee Jones) for not fully embracing his son, Newt, by granting him his name. Although Call's toughness and refusal to admit errors are portrayed as faults, they do not keep him from being known as a "man of vision," one whose undeveloped humanity is, to be sure, intricately intertwined with this vision. *Lonesome Dove* is unique for achieving, within the confines of the neoconservative TV western, a narrative that admits to the failures of the male as fully developed human being by way of showing his failure as domestic creature. The responsible father of *The Rifleman*, the man of many consolations in an earlier moment, has been exposed, as have the consequences of the frontier experience. *Lonesome Dove* and *Salmonberries*, two very different works concerned with the frontier at different phases of its conquest, may be counted as among the key westerns, certainly for their remarks on the consequences of the American conquest and for their ability to point a new way for civilization outside of patriarchy.

Coda

The Rifleman's final season was marked by a gradual decline that was duly noted by the network. As is often the case with series television, *The Rifleman* began to repeat themes, attempt strained ones, and falter in its otherwise fine production values, causing it to lose its steady grip on top ratings for its time slot. Misjudgments like those associated with the compromised direction of the often extraordinary "Waste," which opened the last season, tended to make the show's deterioration more visible. More serious misjudgments are apparent in giving Lucas a halfhearted love relationship à la

Matt Dillon–Kitty in *Gunsmoke*. The ABC network, Dick Powell, and Levy-Gardner-Laven made the 1963 season the final chapter of *The Rifleman*, bringing to an end a show that was part of the era's ongoing poetic elegy for the western.

Chuck Connors died in 1992. Paul Fix died in 1983. Johnny Crawford at this writing heads a dance orchestra in Hollywood. Many of *The Rifleman*'s creators, including Arthur Gardner, Arnold Laven, and Hershel Burke Gilbert, are prospering in happy lives today.

have had a long and problematical relationship with the **105** TV western of the 1950s, and with *The Rifleman*, which I have always felt to be its most interesting and representative example. Here I have discussed the relationship of the TV western to the culture of the 1950s, yet I cannot pretend to do so from some Olympian academic distance.

My personal relationship with the genre and its connections to my life may be worth recounting, not as a series of reminiscences as much as a representative "case study" of the shaping of masculinity by postwar media culture, in particular by action-adventure genres aimed primarily at boys and men.

The TV western very much preoccupied me as a boy growing up in a small town in Pennsylvania during the era. It is now something of a commonplace that television was a major challenge to cinema in the postwar years; what needs further inquiry is the transformation of the relatively social experience of the cinema into the more insulated experience of television, at a time when U.S. society was about to become extremely atomized and alienated, manifested today by the shockingly low percentage—less than half—of eligible voters who bother to register to vote. Concerns about television's negative influence tend, however, to outstrip serious evaluation of early television's artistic contributions. Setting aside Newton Minow's important statement that early television was a "vast wasteland," television of the era seemed to me, then and now, to be almost on a par with late 1950s Hollywood, the quality of television programming far outstripping the debased situation of today. The writing and direction of genre shows like the TV western makes the point. But I could not articulate issues of quality in the late 1950s. The western formed for me a dream of adventure and escape from small-town life; I could not be aware at the time of the extent to which it shaped my views of the masculine self, and some of the most dangerous aspects of the modern patriarchal order, with its gun culture and increasingly devious authority over women. I chose to write this monograph about *The Rifleman* because of the show's legitimate status as a TV milestone. It was indeed an innovative and popular show during its five-year run on ABC television; I was aware of its status, which tended to validate my enjoyment of it as I pursued *Rifleman* collectibles as a youngster. But my connections to the program are more personal, with *The Rifleman* a kind of framing device and, on reflection, a reminder of the delusions of many dominant notions of the United States that are contained in the western.

During the late 1950s my friends and I found toy guns to be our preferred playthings. The toy racks of local department stores prominently featured realistic-looking toy guns. I was especially fond of my two Mattel "Shootin' Shell" revolvers, which closely resembled Colt .45s—the guns even fired small plastic bullets and loaded like a real revolver. I also recall owning a toy Sharps carbine (associated with the murderous U.S. 7th Cavalry in the nineteenth century), a toy sawed-off shotgun derived from the TV western *The Rebel*, and of course

Lucas McCain's "flip special," the toy version of the weapon that Chuck Connors carried on *The Rifleman.*

Before too long, toy guns were replaced with real ones. My father was a lifetime member of the National Rifle Association and a former army officer; firearms were an important part of his sense of self. We were close, our mutual interests partially a shield, I think, from troubled family life, which hardly resembled images from archetypal 1950s sitcoms like *The Adventures of Ozzie and Harriet.* The ludicrousness of the Nelsons as a model family seemed clear to me before I had the vocabulary to say so, given what went on in my own life and the lives of my young pals. Like me, my father had an interest in the Old West that I think explains, in retrospect, my sense of the TV and cinematic western, in their harkening to an imagined America of unbridled male id, as an escape from 1950s repression not afforded by other entertainment genres—sci-fi, the horror film, and melodrama were among the genres often seen as soft-headed and somehow "unmanly," although I amply partook of them all.

My father built a small gun range on my grandmother's large property on the edge of town. We spent many a Saturday afternoon at target practice with my father's small arsenal of rifles and handguns, sometimes debunking the ridiculous shooting feats attributed to historical Wild West figures like Billy the Kid and Wild Bill Hickok, or the even more ludicrous feats of television and movie cowboys.

To my mind, guns, and my father's extraordinary prowess with them (he won any number of championship medals and trophies in his early years), in large part established my father's authority, and I came to see such weapons as a bedrock of masculinity overall. He was a crack shot whom I attempted to surpass; upon doing so in my late teens, that part of our relationship came to an end, as the relationship itself was changing and not for the better. Opposition to my father's conservatism followed from my involvement as a college student in the resistance to the U.S. incursion in Southeast Asia, as did my interest in the civil rights and feminist movements.

With my discovery of feminism I rather belatedly became aware of society's notion of women, which seemed to be an image other than that offered by John Ford and TV westerns like *The Rifleman*. The woman as revered protector of home and hearth of the western and other fiction did not jibe with my practical experience. I found that men more often regarded women as sexual toys or as nuisances to be shunted aside as painlessly (for the male) as possible. Images from the western, from the male culture that I shared with my father in my early years, kept rerunning in my mind. Looking back over my early life, I understand why the 1950s and the period before Vietnam and Watergate have been enshrined as the halcyon moment of "family values" by postmodern conservative culture. That decade, when the government encouraged citizens to lead fantasy lives as reality became oppressive and miserable, is postwar America's outstanding symbol of repression and reaction.

The gun culture of my father's era, always conservative, did impart to me a certain degree of self-discipline and dexterity. It seems rather different in retrospect from what the gun culture has become today. The modern gun lobby has obvious ideological and financial agendas that allow no argument, unconcerned as it is about, and tending to obfuscate, the extraordinary destructive power of guns (we must be honest—their purpose is to kill), their role in the mythology of violence in the United States, and their formative effect on the consciousness of so many disaffected, alienated young people. Their violence is always marked as aberrant and "criminal," of course, in contrast to the sanctioned violence of the state as it pursues the aims of corporate capitalism.

The play world of toy guns that I knew in the 1950s soon showed its other face, the gun violence of the 1960s, with its political assassinations and, most especially, the war in Vietnam. Memoirs of the period by writer-veterans such as Ron Kovic (*Born on the Fourth of July*) and Michael Herr (*Dispatches*) underscore the disparity between fantasies of violence projected by pop culture of the 1950s and violence that suddenly is the real thing. Along with other traumas surrounding the war and its consequences for the United States and the world, the steady fixation on, and misrepresentation of, gun violence formed a significant lie of the epoch.

At this writing, the Colt Armory, a sprawling, decaying factory complex on the edge of Hartford, Connecticut, sits abandoned, waiting to be transformed into an office-and-shopping mall. The site, not far from my current home, is a perfect symbol of postindustrial America. In a city with one of the highest poverty rates in the country, its downtown corporate citadel framed by acres of urban blight, the complex created by Samuel Colt might be seen as representing the consequences of the genocide that won the West, accomplished in part with deadly Colt .45 Peacemakers. The massive pre– and post–Civil War violence, largely against Hispanics, Native Americans, and African Americans, has echoes today in the race and class polarization of the United States. Today, the ethic of the frontier conquest, long internalized by generations of our citizens, is playing its endgame in the desperation of a socially and economically unjust nation.

The Rifleman is a superbly well-realized, innovative, but idealized story of a father-son relationship, located as much in a fanciful postwar America as in a fanciful frontier America. Watching the series now, I look back, less with nostalgia than with considerable anguish, sadness, and anger, at what it means, then and now, to be a boy and man in the United States under patriarchal capitalism. The unconditional love

109

shared by Lucas McCain and his son, Mark, seems plausible to me; there were many times when I felt such as child and adult. What is so vexing are the unexamined aspects of this relationship, the questions not asked of father or son, the uninterrogated narrative of fatherhood and the fathering of America.

PRODUCTION HISTORY

Source: Tim Brooks and Earle Marsh, *The Complete Directory to Prime Time Network TV Shows*, 1946–, 3rd ed. (New York: Ballantine, 1985), 713.

Telecasts

First: September 30, 1958
Last: July 1, 1963

Broadcast History

Season	Network	Time
Sept. 1958–Sept. 1960	ABC	Tuesday 9:00–9:30
Sept. 1960–Sept. 1961	ABC	Tuesday 8:00–8:30
Oct. 1961–July 1963	ABC	Monday 8:30–9:00

Cast

Lucas McCain	Chuck Connors
Mark McCain	Johnny Crawford
Marshal Micah	Paul Fix
Millie Scott	Joan Taylor
Lou Mallory	Patricia Blair
Sweeney	Bill Quinn
Hattie Denton	Hope Summers

Produced by Jules Levy, Arthur Gardner, and Arnold Laven for Four Star Television. Directed by Arnold Laven, Sam Peckinpah, Joseph H. Lewis, Ida Lupino, Tom Gries, Ted Post, Richard Donner, Lewis Allen, others. Music by Hershel Burke Gilbert.

Source: TV Tome, "The Rifleman—Episode List," http://www.tvtome.com/tv-tome/servlet/EpisodeGuideServlet/showid-1669/The_Rifleman (accessed April 21, 2005).

Episode no.	Prod no.	Original Air Date	Episode Title
		Season 1	
1. 1-1	8438	30 September 1958	The Sharpshooter
2. 1-2	6203	7 September 1958	Home Ranch
3. 1-3	6205	14 October 1958	End of a Young Gun
4. 1-4	6211	21 October 1958	The Marshal
5. 1-5	6207	28 October 1958	The Brother-in-Law
6. 1-6	6219	4 November 1958	Eight Hours to Die
7. 1-7	6213	11 November 1958	Duel of Honor
8. 1-8	6223	8 October 1958	The Safe Guard
9. 1-9	6217	25 November 1958	The Sister
10. 1-10	6215	26 December 1958	New Orleans Menace
11. 1-11	6209	9 December 1958	The Apprentice Sheriff
12. 1-12	6229	16 December 1958	Young Englishman
13. 1-13	6201	23 December 1958	The Angry Gun
14. 1-14	6233	30 December 1958	The Gaucho
15. 1-15	6231	6 January 1959	The Pet
16. 1-16	6221	13 January 1959	The Sheridan Story

Episode no.	Prod no.	Air Date	Episode Title
17. 1-17	6227	20 January 1959	The Retired Gun
18. 1-18	6225	27 January 1959	The Photographer
19. 1-19	6237	3 February 1959	Shivaree
20. 1-20	6241	10 February 1959	The Deadeye Kid
21. 1-21	62391	7 February 1959	The Indian
22. 1-22	6235	24 February 1959	The Boarding House
23. 1-23	6245	30 March 1959	The Second Witness
24. 1-24	6243	10 March 1959	The Trade
25. 1-25	6247	17 March 1959	One Went to Denver
26. 1-26	6249	24 March 1959	The Deadly Wait
27. 1-27	6251	31 March 1959	The Wrong Man
28. 1-28	6253	7 April 1959	The Challenge
29. 1-29	6257	14 April 1959	The Hawk
30. 1-30	6261	21 April 1959	Three-Legged Terror
31. 1-31	6263	28 April 1959	The Angry Man
32. 1-32	6259	5 May 1959	The Woman
33. 1-33	6265	12 May 1959	The Money Gun
34. 1-34	6269	19 May 1959	A Matter of Faith
35. 1-35	6271	26 May 1959	Blood Brothers
36. 1-36	6273	20 June 1959	Stranger at Night
37. 1-37	6267	9 June 1959	The Raid
38. 1-38	6275	16 June 1959	Outlaw's Inheritance
39. 1-39	6277	23 June 1959	Boomerang
40. 1-40	6279	30 June 1959	The Mind Reader

Season 2

Episode no.	Prod no.	Air Date	Episode Title
41. 2-1	2410	29 September 1959	The Patsy
42. 2-2	2414	6 October 1959	Bloodlines
43. 2-3	2408	13 October 1959	The Blowout
44. 2-4	2412	20 October 1959	Obituary
45. 2-5	2406	27 October 1959	Tension
46. 2-6	2422	3 November 1959	Eddie's Daughter
47. 2-7	2430	10 November 1959	Panic
48. 2-8	2402	17 November 1959	Ordeal
49. 2-9	2424	24 November 1959	The Spiked Rifle
50. 2-10	2404	1 December 1959	Letter of the Law
51. 2-11	2428	8 December 1959	The Legacy
52. 2-12	2416	15 December 1959	The Baby Sitter
53. 2-13	2418	22 December 1959	The Coward

Episode no.	Prod no.	Air Date	Episode Title
54. 2-14	2434	29 December 1959	Surveyors
55. 2-15	2438	5 January 1960	Day of the Hunter
56. 2-16	2436	12 January 1960	Mail Order Groom
57. 2-17	2440	19 January 1960	A Case of Identity
58. 2-18	2442	26 January 1960	The Visitors
59. 2-19	2432	2 February 1960	The Hero
60. 2-20	2444	9 February 1960	The Horse Traders
61. 2-21	2448	16 February 1960	The Spoiler
62. 2-22	2450	23 February 1960	Heller
63. 2-23	2446	1 March 1960	The Grasshopper
64. 2-24	2458	8 March 1960	A Time for Singing
65. 2-25	2454	15 March 1960	The Deserter
66. 2-26	2420	22 March 1960	The Vision
67. 2-27	2452	29 March 1960	The Lariat
68. 2-28	2464	5 April 1960	Smoke Screen
69. 2-29	2462	12 April 1960	Shotgun Man
70. 2-30	2468	19 April 1960	Sins of the Father
71. 2-31	2456	26 April 1960	The Prodigal
72. 2-32	2472	3 May 1960	The Fourflusher
73. 2-33	2476	10 May 1960	The Jailbird
74. 2-34	2478	17 May 1960	Meeting at Midnight
75. 2-35	2480	24 May 1960	Nora
76. 2-36	2482	31 May 1960	The Hangman

Season 3

Episode no.	Prod no.	Air Date	Episode Title
77. 3-1	3501	27 September 1960	Trail of Hate
78. 3-2	2470	4 October 1960	Woman from Hog Ridge
79. 3-3	2460	11 October 1960	Seven
80. 3-4	3521	18 September 1960	The Pitchman
81. 3-5	3515	25 October 1960	Strange Town
82. 3-6	3505	1 November 1960	Baranca
83. 3-7	3511	8 November 1960	The Martinet
84. 3-8	3535	15 November 1960	Miss Milly
85. 3-9	3513	22 November 1960	Dead Cold Cash
86. 3-10	3509	29 November 1960	The Schoolmaster
87. 3-11	3533	6 December 1960	The Promoter
88. 3-12	3503	13 December 1960	The Illustrator
89. 3-13	3507	20 December 1960	The Silent Knife

Episode no.	Prod no.	Air Date	Episode Title
90. 3-14	3547	27 December 1960	Miss Bertie
91. 3-15	3517	30 January 1961	Six Years and a Day
92. 3-16	3531	10 January 1961	Flowers by the Door
93. 3-17	3523	17 January 1961	Long Trek
94. 3-18	3519	24 January 1961	The Actress
95. 3-19	3535	31 January 1961	Face of Yesterday
96. 3-20	3551	7 February 1961	The Wyoming Story (1)
97. 3-21	3553	14 February 1961	The Wyoming Story (2)
98. 3-22	3541	21 February 1961	Closer Than a Brother
99. 3-23	3561	28 February 1961	The Lost Treasure of Canyon Town
100. 3-24	3559	7 March 1961	Dark Day at North Fork
101. 3-25	3565	14 March 1961	The Prisoner
102. 3-26	3563	21 March 1961	Assault
103. 3-27	3543	28 March 1961	Short Rope for a Tall Man
104. 3-28	3537	4 April 1961	The Clarence Bibs Story
105. 3-29	3555	11 April 1961	The Score Is Even
106. 3-30	3549	18 April 1961	The Mescalaro Curse
107. 3-31	3569	25 April 1961	Stopover
108. 3-32	3529	2 May 1961	The Lonesome Ride
109. 3-33	3545	9 May 1961	Death Trap
110. 3-34	3567	16 May 1961	The Queue

Season 4

Episode no.	Prod no.	Air Date	Episode Title
111. 4-1	4804	2 October 1961	The Vaqueros
112. 4-2	4816	9 October 1961	First Wages
113. 4-3	4810	16 September 1961	Sheer Terror
114. 4-4	4806	23 October 1961	The Stand-In
115. 4-5	4814	30 October 1961	The Journey Back
116. 4-6	4828	6 November 1961	The Decision
117. 4-7	4824	13 November 1961	Knight Errant
118. 4-8	4818	20 November 1961	Honest Abe
119. 4-9	4830	27 November 1961	The Long Goodbye
120. 4-10	4822	4 December 1961	The Shattered Idol
121. 4-11	4812	11 December 1961	Long Gun from Tucson
122. 4-12	4840	18 December 1961	The High Country
123. 4-13	4808	25 December 1961	A Friend in Need
124. 4-14	4826	1 January 1962	Skull

Episode no.	Prod no.	Air Date	Episode Title
125. 4-15	4844	8 January 1962	The Princess
126. 4-16	4802	15 January 1962	Gunfire
127. 4-17	4848	22 January 1962	The Quiet Fear
128. 4-18	4850	29 January 1962	Sporting Chance
129. 4-19	4832	5 February 1962	A Young Man's Fancy
130. 4-20	4820	12 February 1962	The Man from Salinas
131. 4-21	4852	19 February 1962	Two Ounces of Tin
132. 4-22	4846	26 February 1962	Deadly Image
133. 4-23	4854	5 March 1962	The Debt
134. 4-24	4856	12 March 1962	The Tinhorn
135. 4-25	4842	19 March 1962	None So Blind
136. 4-26	4842	26 March 1962	Jealous Man
137. 4-27	4838	2 April 1962	Guilty Conscience
138. 4-28	4860	9 April 1962	Day of Reckoning
139. 4-29	4862	16 April 1962	The Day a Town Slept
140. 4-30	4864	23 April 1962	Milly's Brother
141. 4-31	4866	30 April 1962	Outlaw's Shoes
142. 4-32	4868	7 May 1962	The Executioner

Season 5

Episode no.	Prod no.	Air Date	Episode Title
143. 5-1	5202	1 October 1962	Waste (1)
144. 5-2	5204	8 October 1962	Waste (2)
145. 5-3	5206	15 October 1962	Lou Mallory
146. 5-4	5220	22 October 1962	Quiet Night, Deadly Night
147. 5-5	5226	29 October 1962	Death Never Rides Alone
148. 5-6	5234	5 November 1962	I Take This Woman
149. 5-7	5222	12 November 1962	The Assailants
150. 5-8	5228	19 November 1962	Mark's Rifle
151. 5-9	5232	26 November 1962	The Most Amazing Man
152. 5-10	5218	3 December 1962	Squeeze Play
153. 5-11	5236	10 December 1962	Gun Shy
154. 5-12	5212	17 December 1962	The Anvil Chorus
155. 5-13	5214	24 December 1962	Conflict
156. 5-14	5240	7 January 1963	Incident at Line Shack Six
157. 5-15	5210	14 January 1963	Suspicion
158. 5-16	5242	21 January 1963	The Sidewinder
159. 5-17	5230	28 January 1962	The Sixteenth Cousin

Episode no.	Prod no.	Air Date	Episode Title
160. 5-18	5224	4 February 1963	Hostages to Fortune
161. 5-19	5250	11 February 1963	And the Devil Makes Five
162. 5-20	5248	18 February 1963	End of the Hunt
163. 5-21	5244	25 February 1963	The Bullet
164. 5-22	5254	4 March 1963	Requiem at Mission Springs
165. 5-23	5256	11 March 1963	The Guest
166. 5-24	5262	18 March 1963	Old Man Running (aka The Wanted Man)
167. 5-25	5246	1 April 1963	Which Way'd They Go?
168. 5-26	5216	8 April 1963	Old Tony

Introduction

1. Michele Hilmes, *Only Connect: A Cultural History of Broadcasting in the United States* (Belmont, CA: Wadsworth, 2002).

2. For a discussion of this crisis, see William Boddy, *Fifties TV: The Industry and Its Critics* (Urbana: University of Illinois Press, 1990), 215–33.

3. Hilmes, *Only Connect*, 200.

4. Boddy, *Fifties TV*, 146–47.

5. This concept has been discussed in numerous works on Ford. For a recent work, see Thomas Schatz, "*Stagecoach* and Hollywood's 'A' Western Renaissance," in *John Ford's Stagecoach*, ed. Barry Keith Grant (New York: Cambridge University Press, 2002), 21–47. There are many discussions of *Stagecoach* in Gaylyn Studlar and Matthew Bernstein, eds., *John Ford Made Westerns: Filming the Legend in the Sound Era* (Bloomington: Indiana University Press, 2001). See in particular the essay by Robin Wood, "Shall We Gather at the River? The Late Films of John Ford," 23–41.

6. The role of television in postwar life is discussed in Karal Ann Marling, *As Seen on TV: The Visual Culture of Everyday Life in the 1950s* (Cambridge, MA: Harvard University Press, 1994).

7. Hilmes, *Only Connect*, 200. Slightly different figures are offered in Ronald Jackson, *Classic TV Westerns* (New York: Citadel, 1994). The small difference in the count of adult TV westerns at their peak de-

pends largely on arguments about the number of westerns quickly scrapped on release.

8. Richard Slotkin, *Gunfighter Nation: The Myth of the Frontier in Twentieth-Century America* (New York: Atheneum, 1992), 348.

9. The quote can be found in various sources, including Gore Vidal, *The American Presidency* (Berkeley, CA: Odonian, 1998), 52.

10. A good sketch of the period is Marty Jezer, *The Dark Ages: Life in the U.S., 1945–1960* (Boston: South End, 1980).

11. See Slotkin, *Gunfighter Nation*, for a discussion of the "gunfighter" style of the CIA, 442–516.

12. Elizabeth Fones-Wolf, *Selling Free Enterprise: The Business Assault on Labor and Liberalism, 1945–1960* (Urbana: University of Illinois Press, 1994).

13. An illuminating book on the western's context in the Cold War is Stanley Corkin, *Cowboys as Cold Warriors: The Western and U.S. History* (Philadelphia: Temple University Press, 2004).

14. A view offered by Fones-Wolf in her discussion of the use of persuasion by corporate power in the postwar era in *Selling Free Enterprise*. See esp. 33–35, 52–53.

15. This ideology is developed in Peter Biskind, *Seeing Is Believing: How Hollywood Taught Us to Stop Worrying and Love the Fifties* (New York: Pantheon, 1983).

16. Although the integrity of its scholarship has been disputed, it seems to me there is much worthwhile in Michael Bellesiles's *Arming America: The Origins of a National Gun Culture* (New York: Alfred A. Knopf, 2000), in particular its arguments about the postbellum sale of guns and the gun industry's impact on today's society.

17. See Barry Keith Grant, "Spokes in the Wheel," in *John Ford's Stagecoach*, ed. Grant, 1–20.

18. See Hilmes, *Only Connect*, 200.

19. For a discussion of the Earp-Clanton stories and their connections to the "terrible clan," see William Luhr, "Reception, Representation, and the O.K. Corral: Shifting Images of Wyatt Earp," in *Authority and Transgression in Literature and Film*, ed. Bonnie Braendlin and Hans Braendlin (Tallahassee: Florida State University Press, 1996), 23–45.

20. The relevance of the notion of the Organization Man and his need for escapism is discussed in Marling, *As Seen on TV*. Central to Marling's work is David Riesman, Nathan Glazer, and Reuel Denney, *The Lonely Crowd: A Study of the Changing American Character*

(New Haven, CT: Yale University Press, 1950). This work discusses, among other issues, the inverted, hobby-oriented nature of postwar men as they sensed their increased ineffectuality in the public arena.

21. According to Marling, in *As Seen on TV*, the need for escapism was a concern for the postwar centrists. See Arthur Schlesinger, Jr., "The Crisis in American Masculinity," *Esquire*, November 1958, pp. 64–66.

22. Slotkin discusses variations in gunfighter and other themes of the western in *Gunfighter Nation*. See esp. 347–49.

23. Hilmes, *Only Connect*, 200.

24. Johnny Crawford, interview by author, October 4, 2002.

25. Biskind, *Seeing Is Believing*, 291.

26. Arnold Laven, interview by author, October 21, 2002.

27. Hartland Plastics produced a figure of Lucas McCain, armed with his rifle and mounted on a chestnut horse, that has sold on eBay for as much as $500. Hubley's toy version of McCain's rifle has sold for similar amounts.

28. Marling discusses television-generated consumer goods aimed at girls and women in *As Seen on TV*, 10–49.

29. Laven interview, October 21, 2002.

Chapter 1

1. Laven interview, October 21, 2002.

2. An important account of Peckinpah's television work, to which I am much indebted, is David Weddle, "*If They Move . . . Kill 'Em*": *The Life and Times of Sam Peckinpah* (New York: Grove, 1994), 144–83. Another important account of this phase of Peckinpah's work is Paul Seydor, *Peckinpah: The Western Films* (Urbana: University of Illinois Press, 1980), 3–18.

3. Laven interview, October 26, 2002.

4. Ibid.

5. Ibid.

6. Weddle, "*If They Move . . . Kill 'Em*," 150.

7. Ibid.

8. Laven interview, October 21, 2002.

9. Weddle, "*If They Move . . . Kill 'Em*," 152.

10. Ibid., 151.

11. Laven interview, October 21, 2002.

12. Robert Culp, interview by author, October 14, 2002.

Chapter 2

1. The central work is Arthur Schlesinger, Jr., *The Vital Center: The Politics of Freedom* (New York: Doubleday, 1948). Biskind also discusses the corporate liberal philosophy at length in *Seeing Is Believing*, 10–43.

2. Schlesinger, *Vital Center*, 37.

3. Disney offered one of many images of the West that countered the stifling conformism of postwar life with a dream of adventure. See Robert G. Athearn, *The Mythic West in Twentieth-Century America* (Lawrence: University of Kansas Press), 135–37. On Disney and the Crockett craze, see Paul Anderson, *The Davy Crockett Craze: A Look at the 1950s Phenomenon* (Hillside, IL: R&G, 1996). On Davy Crockett, Disneyland, and *The Wonderful World of Disney*, see J. P. Telotte's *Disney TV* (Detroit: Wayne State University Press, 2004) in the TV Milestones series.

4. Gloria Jahoda, *The Trail of Tears: The Story of the American Indian Removals, 1813–1855* (New York: Wings, 1975), 13–14, 65–66.

5. Culp interview.

6. Slotkin discusses the theme in *Gunfighter Nation*, 461–63.

7. Numerous accounts of the singer-actor's life and career have commented on his embrace in the 1960s and 1970s of both black power and Richard Nixon.

Chapter 3

1. According to Todd McCarthy, Hawks made *Rio Bravo* after noticing the western's preeminence on television. See Todd McCarthy, *Howard Hawks: The Grey Fox of Hollywood* (New York: Grove, 1997), 548.

2. Wilhelm Stekel, *Sexual Aberrations* (New York: Liveright Books, 1930), 117.

Chapter 4

1. Robin Wood, "Man(n) of the West(ern)," *Cineaction* 46 (July 1998): 26–34.

2. John Walker, ed., *Halliwell's Filmgoer's and Video Viewer's Companion*, 10th ed. (New York: HarperCollins, 1993), 181.

3. David Schmoeller, director's commentary track, *Tourist Trap*, DVD, directed by David Schmoeller (1979; Port Washington, NY: Koch Full Moon Releasing, 2002).

4. Ibid.

INDEX

Page numbers in bold refer to illustrations

* 120 source

10 distinction from Western, group as safety, professionalism for protection; men forced out by draft find chaos of war often uncomfortable

2
3.10
4.20